Purpose Driven
FREE TO BE UNAPOLOGETICALLY ME

This book is the work of non-fiction based on my own real-life personal experiences and my memories of them. To protect anonymity, in some instances, I have changed the names of individuals, places, and some identifying details to protect their privacy and identity.

This book is not intended as a substitute for medical advice of physicians. The reader should regularly consult a physician in matters relating to his/ her mental or physical health and particularly respect to any symptoms that may require diagnosis or medical attention. Also if you or someone you know is struggling with thoughts of suicide please seek help right away and call:

**The National Suicide Prevention Lifeline at
1-800-273-8255**

The religious views and opinions expressed in this book are based on the author's personal Christian beliefs and experiences and are not meant to undermine anyone's own religious preference or beliefs thereof.

Unless otherwise indicated, all Scripture quotations are taken from The Holy Bible, New Living Translation Second Edition, copyright © 1996, 2004. Used by permission of Tyndale House Publishers, Inc., Carol Stream, Illinois 60188. All rights reserved.

Copyright © 2020 by Bernadette M. Padgett- All Rights Reserved.
No part of this publication may be reproduced or used in any manner or transmitted in any form or by any means including photocopying for recording, or by any information storage and retrieval system without written permission of the copyright owner/author of this book.

For more information, contact:
Bmariebooks777@gmail.com

Printed in the United States of America
Second paperback edition 2020

Published by: B's Book Bouquet LLC
Website address: www.bsbookbouquetllc.com

ISBN 9780578729862 paperback

Book covers designed by Scott Brody

purpose driven
free to be unapologetically me

A Poetic Autobiography
Based on My True Life Story

Bernadette Marie Padgett

"A New Book Is Blooming"
B's Book Bouquet LLC
© Copyright 2020. All Rights Reserved

Peoria, AZ

Dedication

I dedicate this book to every suffering addict, mentally afflicted, lost, lonely soul; to everyone who has ever felt misunderstood, alone, and forgotten. To those who struggle with their identity, and their place in the world. To the one's like me who are dreamers, writers, artists, and anyone striving to overcome, and has suffered loss. To the ones who feel invisible, broken, disheartened, and feel like giving up- Don't! I encourage you to read this book in hopes you can relate and find hope amidst the pain.

I also dedicate this book to my mother Kathryn. Even though we don't always see eye-to-eye, she has been my rock, and I am forever thankful!

A special dedication to my daughter, Madeline, whom I love with all my heart! I dreamed of her before I ever knew I was pregnant with her. Her spirit was letting me know she was there, and she is the best thing to ever happen to me! I am a proud mommy, and I pray to leave behind my legacy of hope and purpose to believe in yourself and chase after your dreams! And when in doubt, fight your greatest battles on your knees, because in that will be your greatest victory!

Lastly, I dedicate this book to my sweet, courageous Aunt Bernice, who was a true fighter! Because of her belief in me, her willingness to always lend an ear, her inner beauty, and the love she gave me as if I was her own child, I dedicate this book to her. She is no longer with us, but I cherish her spirit and she is dearly missed. I also dedicate this book to all my friends who have passed on. You are my angels in Heaven!

The Lord is close to the brokenhearted; he rescues those whose spirits are crushed.

Psalm 34:18, NLT

O Lord, how long will you forget me? Forever?
How long will you look the other way?

How long must I struggle with anguish in my soul?
With sorrow in my heart every day?

How long will my enemy have the upper hand?
Turn and answer me, O Lord my God!

Restore the sparkle to my eyes, or I will die!
Don't let my enemies gloat, saying, "We have defeated him!"
Don't let them rejoice at my downfall.

But I trust in your unfailing love
I will rejoice because you have rescued me.

I will sing to the Lord because he is good to me.

Psalm 13:1-6, NLT

Acknowledgments

First and foremost, I'd like to thank God for making my dreams come true! He never gave up on me, and I am forever thankful to my Lord and Savior!

Secondly, I'd like to thank all the people who have supported me on my journey, who always believed in me and my talents, and loved me no matter what! *My mother Kathryn, my Aunt Bernice, Aunt Jody, my best friend Cody, and my daughter Madeline.* From the bottom of my heart, thank you all for loving me even at times I wasn't so lovable!

Last but not least, I'd like to thank the Purpose & Passion tour event, which thrust me into my divine destiny where I said 'yes' to God, my destiny, and my dream of writing my book and becoming a published author!

I believe there is a timing for everything, and one door always leads to another!

x

Foreword

To My Daughter Bernadette,

I love you and am so proud of you! Throughout the years, from 17 years old on, when we found out about your mental illness I have seen you suffer a great deal. As I watched you battle your illness, I too have suffered with you.

You have an incredible amount of strength and a desire to succeed. Your poetry has always moved me, and I believe it is what helped you through the many tragedies you faced in your life.

Your talent is a gift from God and contributed to giving you hope and seeing the impossible - like your desire to see rainbows in the night sky! Maybe that rainbow at night is you and your spirit that God has given you which has always pushed you to higher levels.

I always said you would one day write your book, and helped encourage you to put your poetry together and write your story to help others. All your life, I have seen you with the desire to give back; even amidst your own struggles and pain, you were never too far away to lend an ear to someone else who needed you.

Bernadette you are such an inspiration to so many people who can't find the words to describe how they feel. You have given them a voice of understanding! I am very proud of you for writing your book and always knew one day I would see it in book stores throughout the world! I see you writing many more books and leaving your legacy of hope to your little girl. But, more importantly, I see you leaving her with the understanding that strength comes from within and the help of our Lord.

Congratulations!

*Love,
Mom*

Contents

- *Dedication* — v
- *Bible Verses, NLT* — vii
- *Acknowledgments* — ix
- *Foreword* — xi-xii
- *Introduction* — xv

Chapters

1. *Childhood Narrative* — 1
2. *Year 2001/Recovery & Hope* — 9
   (Drug Rehabilitation)
3. *Year 2002/Rehab Again* — 31
4. *Year 2002-2005/Isolation* — 49
5. *Year 2002-2005/Mental Affliction* — 53
   (Bipolar Disorder)
6. *Year 2005-2006/Still Dreaming of Love* — 57
7. *Year 2006/The Relapse* — 63
8. *Year 2008/Long Suffering, Waiting on Love* — 65
9. *Year 2008/Choosing Accountability* — 73
10. *Year 2009/Battling Obesity* — 75
    (Longing for Love-Continues)
11. *Year 2011/Battling Obesity* — 83
    (Weight loss Journey-Continues)
12. *Year 2013/Overcoming Life's Challenges* — 93
13. *Year 2014/Life Event-* — 97
    (Birth of my Daughter Madeline)
14. *Year 2015/Hope, Letting Go, Loneliness Returns* — 101

Contents *(Cont'd)*

Chapters

15. Year 2016/Victor — 103

16. Year 2017-2019/Toby — 107
(A Complicated Love Story)

17. Year 2019/What Matters Most — 121

18. Year 2020/Purpose Driven — 135

Introduction

"Purpose Driven/Free to Be Unapologetically Me"

This is a poetic autobiography put into chronological order based on the time the events and poems were written and took place, and arranged based on grouped subject matter. A narrative describing the trials I faced at the time the poems were written precedes each section of poems.

This book is a creative expression, and purposeful compilation of personal poetry based on my own real-life struggles with drug addiction, mental illness, obesity, isolation, and heartache, while on a spiritual journey to find my God-given, life-long purpose driven by God's mercy and grace and a quest for true love.

My hope is to inspire and strengthen each reader to never give up hope, know without a doubt they are not alone, and remind them miracles do happen!

purpose driven
free to be unapologetically me

1

Childhood Narrative

I was born and raised in Phoenix, AZ, to my single mother, Kathryn Padgett. My father was not present at my birth, and continued to be absent throughout my life. I have an older brother two years older to be exact; who come to find out later is my half- brother. The half just pertains to the biological aspect, because as far as I see it, he is my brother. Period.

My brother and I were raised in a very dysfunctional environment. We moved a lot, and my mom dated several different men throughout our childhood. Her first marriage to "Ron" (to keep his real name confidential) was doomed from the start. He had a great sense of humor and, in a lot of ways, was a big kid himself. He loved to cook, and for the most part, played the role of mother and father while my mother worked two and three jobs to provide for us.

I always knew our family was different from my friends at school who seemed to have a more stable home life. I remember feeling scared a lot as a child because my mom and Ron fought often, and he would get physically violent with her. There was always yelling and arguing and over time, I developed severe anxiety and a nervous stomach due to the events I witnessed as a child. I always worried he was going to kill my mommy!

purpose driven/ free to be unapologetically me

I remember when I started kindergarten, I'd walk home from school, and there was always a suspicious van parked just a few houses down from our home. Come to find out later, it was the Feds and our phone was tapped because Ron was a big-time cocaine dealer and kept this hidden from my mother. Many times, I witnessed my step-dad hiding a white powdery substance up in the air vents and cutting open our mattresses to hide his cocaine. One time while our babysitter was cooking us spaghetti, a bunch of cocaine fell from the above range of the stove, so my babysitter exclaimed, "Well, guess we're having pizza for dinner!"

Turns out that by the time I turned six years old, the Feds caught up with Ron, and he was arrested and sent to prison, where he served 12 years. My mother filed for divorce. My mom did the best she could to raise us, and she managed to always take care of our basic needs and keep us in good schools and in nice neighborhoods. The one thing missing was the emotional support I needed, and I grew up feeling very neglected. I didn't experience much affection or feelings of being loved, and I didn't have much mental or emotional security.

To this day, my upbringing has affected my self-esteem, self-worth, and relationships, especially romantic relationships. My mother did the best she could with little support from her family. It was up to her to take care of my brother and I.

Later, when I was around 12 years old she married a man named "Brian." Brian was a hardworking man who was a good provider, and he was one of the only men my mother ever dated that I actually liked. We moved to N. Phoenix right before I started middle school, and we ended up in a nice, brand new two-story home. This provided the stability I always wanted and needed.

Bernadette Padgett

I never felt emotionally close to my mother, so even while things were better for us financially after she married Brian, I still felt alone. I was an introvert throughout school and suffered from anxiety and depression, even though I wasn't aware what was going with me at the time.

Due to depression and anxiety and the exposure to peer pressure from friends experimenting with substances, I found myself experimenting with marijuana and drinking by the 8th grade. This was the start of my long road of debauchery and self- medicating (to be discussed in the later chapters).

By the time I turned 15, an unexpected process server from the courts showed up at our home while my mother and step-dad Brian were in Jamaica celebrating their honeymoon. I then learned who my biological father was. And it was at this point that my brother and I became aware we were only half- related.

I remember being so overwhelmed with the news, and curious about my real father, but I had no idea what to expect. When my mother and step-dad returned from Jamaica, she sat both my brother and I down for a long talk. She told each of us who our real fathers were, and come to find out; both our fathers were unstable and unfit parents.

I did eventually meet my real father, but I didn't take much interest in him because of his unstable lifestyle. I later learned he has a mental illness (bipolar), which was passed onto me. Also to be discussed in more detail in the later chapters. The following poem is about how I felt about myself as a child, to whom I wrote to myself in my adult years…

Bernadette Padgett
Before It All Began
(A Letter to My Adolescent Self)

My Inner Princess

Dear Bernadette,

I know you are afraid, that life around you is frightening and unpredictable. I see you, and I hear you. I hear your cries at night, and I feel your pain. I see your heart suffering tremendously, and while you cry yourself to sleep, you long for someone to come and hold you while you weep. How you long for a kind word and a compassionate soul to sit by your side; to just be near you, while their silent presence makes you feel the most beautiful love and comfort of what compassion brings.

You needed a hand to hold and a reason to believe. Please don't despair, sweet angel, help is near. God knew what you were going to have to face before you were born, and because God is all- loving, he has equipped you with strength, determination, good will, kindness, and compassion for others.

Even though your life is quite the challenge, know this…with every great struggle, there is a tremendous victory to follow. People don't become great without knowing real heartache.

I know when you look in the mirror all you see are flaws and how this world has done you wrong, but God is always here with you, And what you may see as permanent, really is the release of something new! Something groundbreaking, infinitely powerful, purpose- driven, and you are on the brink of your soul's purpose!

purpose driven/ free to be unapologetically me

God will turn our most tragic life experiences and use it, use us, to inspire, comfort, and reach the unreachable. You are blessed with so many gifts and talents. You think on an original plane, and just when the world thinks they've got the best of you, you come through like a warrior and do it in a way that the world can't help but fall in love with you.

I've seen you in action when someone is tormenting you; it would be easy to judge and condemn, but instead, you found compassion for them. You turned what could have been a bitter end into a moment of clarity and new hope. You turn the light on in the dark. You are destined for greatness! You've walked in the dark of night, been surrounded by evil, yet you are a brave and bold soul who has defeated what was meant to harm you. Your enemies have been forced to look in the mirror, and because of your faith in God, he has shed light on those around you.

If he did it before, he will do it again! So rise up, and embrace who you are! A beautiful, kind, gentle soul; full of originality; with creativity, and a colorful, child-like imagination; youthful, inspiring, intelligent, strong, a child of God, healed, capable, confident, attractive, loved, and accepted just as you are!

You are lacking in nothing! You have nothing to fear! You are not the environment you grew up in. Not even close! You have a chance! God's got your back!

So, when you look in the mirror, know you do not lack. You are full of beauty inside and out! Graceful, humble, a princess crowned, and Heaven-bound! Take Jesus by the hand because He is your father and loves you. Just accept the rest and move forward.

This is a triumphant time for you! Embrace it and smile honey! Because you deserve to! I love you, little angel and never stop dreaming or believing. Your dreams will come true, and love is near!

Me at 5 years old

2

Narrative for Year 2001
(Recovery & Hope/Drug Rehabilitation)

2001 was a rough year for me. It was the time my family sought out residential drug treatment for me. I was mixed up with a rough crowd from high school, and my family knew they needed to get me as far away from Arizona as they could.

I had been experimenting with hard drugs since my freshman year of high school. I started out with marijuana, and it escalated to crystal meth, cocaine, LSD, ketamine (Special K), and ecstasy. Eventually, I became an IV heroin addict. My family was torn apart during my junior year of high school when my mother and step- dad Brian filed for divorce. My brother and I had become accustomed to the finer things in life, living in a brand new two-story home and what finally seemed to be a good, stable father figure in our lives.

I had my first experience with outpatient rehab during my sophomore year when I overdosed on LSD and was sent to the hospital at 15 years old. At that point, my mother pulled me out of school to have me go to I.O.P. (Intensive Outpatient), and I ended up getting so far behind in school by my junior year of high school, I dropped out. This is the time my mother and Brian got a divorce and we were forced to move out of our nice home and move in with a family member.

Life had shifted so drastically, and I felt completely lost. I tried to finish high school and started at a charter school. I started noticing signs that something was severely wrong with me at this time. I felt paranoid, and anxious, and my thoughts were going a million miles a minute! I wasn't sleeping, and I just felt off and not myself altogether. My mom was in denial and thought I just didn't want to go to school, so I was still forced to go even though there were signs something was severely wrong with me.

purpose driven/ free to be unapologetically me

I tried several times to tell my mother something wasn't right, and finally, she took me to a psychiatrist. I was diagnosed with bipolar disorder. She was uneducated about what this disorder was and how I ended up with it, so she reached out to my biological father to find out if he knew anything about the illness. And sure enough he too has bipolar disorder.

My doctor tried different medications on me to see what would help me the most, but nothing seemed to work. Finally, I felt I had no choice. I'll never forget meeting my mother at a sub shop, sitting her down, and telling her I was going to try heroin. A group of friends from high school were experimenting with the drug. My mother tried her hardest to talk me out of it, but I had already made up my mind.

This led to a seven year run of IV drug use with heroin and cocaine, along with some recovery periods in between in which I went to rehab in California in 2001 at New Life. The only thing I felt was working for me to make me feel "normal" at the time was the heroin. I never wanted to become a heroin addict; I mean, realistically, who does? I was self-medicating and became extremely addicted to the point that it was no longer a choice. It was what I needed to get up every day to be able to function.

The following poems reflect my experiences in recovery, which involve two different love stories both Kaleb and Heath. The poems also reflect how I was feeling at the time of recovery, my desire for true love, and also my feelings of hopelessness that lead me to attempt suicide…

Bernadette Padgett
Year 2001/Recovery & Hope
(Heath)

Musician in the Limelight

His presence is like a cool breeze
Yet incredibly warm, and full of light
His touch is like a soft rose petal kissing your cheek
The melody he sings deep from his soul
Brings tears of joy to my eyes
Who is this magnificent being?
How did I ever end up crossing his path?
I feel so warm and happy just daydreaming
Of his calm and incredibly talented nature
He is like an angel to me.
His humor and unique personality makes me want
To cuddle him like a teddy bear.
He is forever in my heart, and always in my prayers
I love you magnificent music man
Heath

purpose driven/ free to be unapologetically me

Bernadette Padgett
Year 2001/Recovery & Hope

Loving Life

Love is such a beautiful thing
Can you believe it's just so foreign to me?
It's so amazing the way God moves through me
His spirit is setting me free!
All the while, I get to see such incredible things
The miraculous sky shining above me
I wait, and listen for my creator to call upon me
Is this heaven? Or is this earth?
Wait; I think it's both
I am so lucky to be here!
I wonder what will happen next.
Maybe I'll get to experience the look of love
A tear of joy
The happiness so high above
One thing I must remember is to live each moment
Like it's forever!

purpose driven/ free to be unapologetically me

Bernadette Padgett
2001/Recovery & Hope

Spirituality

Spirituality is the key
It reminds me of how I felt at my most desperate
Moments and how something was always
Looking out for me
It reminds me to pray when I'm in need
I'm in awe at how easy it can be
To simply just love me
When I can do that it allows me
To love you immediately
How awesome the days can be
To just sit and look at you whole-heartedly
Love never has to end, especially when
You're being a true friend

2001/ Recovery & Hope

Finding the Balance

I realize I can be overly sensitive, but I am praying I can learn not to internalize everything that happens to me and not take it too personally. To learn to be assertive with my feelings and not stuff it down; to express my desires and learn how to communicate them without being aggressive or demanding.

I know I can do this because I have God in my life and he loves me unconditionally through and through. I believe I will have brighter days ahead. But right now, even though I'm not feeling totally ecstatic about life, at least I can take comfort knowing I'm working on myself and preparing to be able to live an awesome life, full of love, peace, happiness, and self-respect simply by working on me, step by step.

Bernadette Padgett
2001/Drug Rehabilitation

Suffering in Silence

I hate this place, this awful dreaded place!
I am in so much gloom
All I feel is doom!
I fear it will tear me to bits!
No matter how horrible things may get,
There has got to be a way out!
Some glimmer of hope and inspiration
I can't decide whether I want to live or die
Oh how I wish there could be some sunshine
Now you feel me trying to hold on,
Never wanting to live alone
Although I do feel so alone
Please God help me to want to try
Before I die!

purpose driven/ free to be unapologetically me

2001/ Drug Rehabilitation

The Struggle

Life can be so torturous when
Things don't go my way
Everything surrounding me is why I want to change.
People think I'm strange
Because I go astray
But, in all actuality it's them that do the same.
When the feeling of loneliness
Hits me like a train,
It's you I'll come running to
To get me out of pain!

Bernadette Padgett
2001/Drug Rehabilitation
(Stumbled Upon Love) "Kaleb"

My Fantasy about Kaleb

I feel the music and the beat
Its powerful sound sweeps me off my feet
It rushes through me week after week
Color all around surrounds me like a dream
A feeling of unity for everyone to keep
I make eye contact with the one that
Makes those records go round
That powerful stare lets me know he cares
Because in my heart he's forever there
We join hand- in- hand with
The club kids all around And as we
Dance the night away we know
This is true love we
Have found!

purpose driven/ free to be unapologetically me

2001/ Drug Rehabilitation
(Stumbled Upon Love) "Kaleb"

Forbidden Love

I can't recall the first moment I realized how true this love really was. I guess you could say it was love at first sight. From the second I laid eyes on him, my heart skipped a beat. I was weak all over, and my breath caught in my chest. Who I'm speaking of is my dearest love, Kaleb.

We met in California due to some unpleasant circumstances for the both of us at the time. We both had gone through similar trials in life. Although our circumstances were not ideal, I was pleased to know we both had an opportunity for a fresh start.

Who knew this would lead to meeting a soul-mate? Infatuation? Maybe…all I knew was this man spoke to my heart, and I saw myself in him. When we exchanged glances and smiles I saw the male version of me staring back.

There was a house for the guys and one for the girls. The only thing separating us was the wall in between. Well, and of course, the staff who kept us apart because fraternizing wasn't allowed. "Too early for love" was what my sponsor would say. I was court-ordered to be there, so there wasn't much room to flirt, or build a relationship with the opposite sex.

I was there to get my life on track and get sober; however, I did not expect that God had other plans for me. I wanted a new beginning and a second chance at happiness.

How lucky Kaleb and I were that our lives had crossed paths. Some people go their entire life and never find a love like this.
It was truly electrifying!

Bernadette Padgett
2001/ Drug Rehabilitation
(Stumbled Upon Love) "Kaleb"

We were so young and both of us were miles from home. Neither of us had any family around, but I was determined to find a new family to call my own. Kaleb was the one with whom I wanted to share my life.

I had no idea what an emotional roller coaster ride I would embark upon. All I knew was I will cherish this love I experienced for a lifetime!

Going back to the moment Kaleb and I first met; we had a meeting at the girl's house, guys and girls together. We all gathered in the living room about to have a discussion on hope vs. faith. I was sitting next to Rita, who introduced me to Kaleb. Rita excitedly exclaimed, "Kaleb, this is Bernadette! She's family!" What she was meant was because Rita, Kaleb, and I all came from the rave scene, so we were really like a family.

Kaleb was from the East Coast; me from the West. I knew from the start this was going to be a challenge since our families were stationed on opposite sides of the country. That's what makes this so ironic. I mean, what were the chances of Kaleb and I meeting when we were from opposite ends of the world.

He was so incredibly attractive; his eyes completely captivated me, and he drew me in with his irresistible smile- so much so that I immediately knew this was true love! He had dark, shaved hair, flawless skin and dark, puppy- dog eyes. His spirit just lit up my life! He had the most gorgeous face I ever seen with remarkable sense of style. There was a glow about him and such a tender love and sweetness that truly was endearing.

After our introduction, we exchanged battle scars as each of us had the same drug of choice. We were recovering from IV heroin addiction. We seemed to instantly have a deep unspoken understanding of one another. After our group discussion, the men and women went their separate ways

The men went back to their house, and the women stayed put. The staff would not let us spend too much time with the opposite sex, for reasons that were obvious. Relationships can be dangerous, and they wanted us to focus on our recovery.

This felt like a major draw- back because here I was just introduced to what I felt was a once –in- a -lifetime kind of love. I shared a room with three other ladies, and I absolutely loved where my bed was located because it overlooked the wall of the men's house just outside the window.

The rehab we were at was very upscale; it was right across from the ocean, and it had a beautiful court- yard with a fountain in the center on the women's side. There were palm trees all around, and often, it felt like more of a vacation than rehab. My mother sold her house to give me a nice place to recover. The cost didn't matter to her because she knew I was there to turn my life around. I just didn't expect I'd find true love in the process.

There was a night in particular I just couldn't sleep. I anxiously anticipated when I'd get to see Kaleb. I woke at 5am to get ready for our 7 am meeting because I wanted to look my best! I was still a little sleepy as we walked down the alley to catch our ride to the meeting. (The guys and girls all met at the end of the same alley).

I saw Kaleb standing there with the other guys and I went right up to him feeling confident and in good spirits and gave him a hug. He seemed tired too. As I gave him a hug, my heart was beating a million miles a minute! I thought to myself that the year 2000 wasn't going to be too bad after all! The meeting was only an hour long and I sat in the back of the room so it wouldn't be obvious I had feelings for him. Each day consisted of a routine; it was highly structured and there was not much personal time.

Bernadette Padgett
2001/ Drug Rehabilitation
(Stumbled Upon Love) "Kaleb"

I've always been a dreamer so any chance I would get I'd fantasize about what life would be like when I left New Life.

I journaled often, usually in the court-yard or in bed before I went to sleep. One particular evening at the beginning of the week. I wrote down some fears I had about moving forward on my own without a chemical crutch. I knew there would be pain along with healing.

It's funny because with the amount of healing I've had to do in my life it's no wonder I was named after the saint of healing, "Saint Bernadette." I have always felt that in my walk through life and drug addiction and all the challenges I have faced, that I was being watched over, that I had God, Jesus, and angels on my side pulling for me and looking after me.

As I sat writing outside in the court-yard, I saw Kaleb was outside, too. I was so thrilled to see him, and we said hi and exchanged smiles. We liked the same type of music, so we exchanged tapes of our favorite DJs. I could never get over Kaleb's smile! He just beamed with light and love! Masculine, but with a pretty-boy type of face too! Just the look I sought out in a man. There was so much more to Kaleb, though, than just a gorgeous face.

He was sincere, heart-felt, and a writer too. I absolutely loved that about him because we were kindred spirits. I love men that can be in touch with their feelings and have an artistic outlet as well. I truly believe it takes creativity and talent to write. Writing just so happened to be one more thing we had in common. After Kaleb and I exchanged hellos, there was so much more I wanted to say, but I was speechless. The words just wouldn't come out.

The chemistry between us, however, was so intense. I was awe-struck, we were inter-connected, and the love I felt was exhilarating! I truly felt we were made-for-each other! I know we had just met, but there was truly something special between us! An epic connection you only dream about in fairytales!

purpose driven/ free to be unapologetically me

So magical and profound, where my spirit had met its match, and I was home. A match made in heaven! I had never felt this for anyone else in my life! This all happened so quickly and I realized that if I feel this he must feel it too! But I needed clarification so I went to one of the ladies in the house Suzy.

She was one of my favorites. She was sweet, honest, and very down-to-earth. She was an older woman and I felt safe confiding in her. I was ready for my confirmation, so one particular Wednesday in January 2001 I went to Suzy and asked if she would get the scoop about how Kaleb felt about me because I was too shy to find out for myself.

I anxiously awaited the news as Suzy snuck over to the guy's side to converse with Kaleb. It only took a few moments and she returned. To my sweet surprise, she explained to me when she approached him with this question he simply smiled and said he was into me too!! I was overjoyed and shrieked with sheer delight!

He gave her a composition book with his poetry writing to give to me, and it was my most cherished possession! (However, I ended up losing it years down the road, which was so heartbreaking!) But now what? The ball was obviously in my court. I proceeded to give Suzy a big hug and thanked her! I went on with my day and my routine, anxiously waiting when I'd be face- to- face with Kaleb again.

New Life was not all fun and games, though. We were on a serious mission to change our lives, and with me being court-ordered to be there, there was a lot riding on my successful completion of the program. If I was kicked out for fraternizing, I would surely land myself in jail. It was no surprise, however, to the staff and residents that Kaleb and I had a thing for each other, so we had to be careful and watch our every step. It got to the point that staff would separate us so that we couldn't even sit next to each other, even though we were following the rules.

Bernadette Padgett
2001/ Drug Rehabilitation
(Stumbled Upon Love) "Kaleb"

Sad, really, but our love was so apparent, they were forced to keep us apart. Just like forbidden love.

Eventually, Kaleb graduated before me and left the house. I was so sad, but I knew we would still see each other at meetings outside the facility. At one point, I remember he asked me out on a date to go check out the Queen Mary when I had my weekends out, but it never happened.

Our lives went on, and eventually I graduated from New Life too. Shortly after, I returned home to Arizona. Kaleb and I spoke on the phone a few times and he remained in California for about another year after graduation.

He eventually moved back to the East Coast and he and I kept in contact over the phone here and there. He ended up marrying and having a son. We lost touch for about 10 years when I finally found him on social media and saw he was married. I was heartbroken! I prayed and cried day and night that he and I would reunite. I reached out to him a couple times online but never heard back until about a year or two later.

At this point, he was divorced and a full- time dad. We spoke on the phone several times, but we were in different places in our lives and a lot of time had gone by. We spoke of making a trip to see each other again someday, but it still hasn't happened.

During the 10- year period where we lost contact, my heart was in such despair. I dreamed of him often, spoke to family and friends about him, longed to hold him. I needed closure. So when we reunited over the phone and online, I was so happy and had high hopes that my dream of marrying him could still come true!

But with life circumstances, our lives being thousands of miles apart and he having a son, it just wasn't possible- or at least that's what we told ourselves. I eventually ended up having a child too. Never married, but happy to have a daughter!

I always dreamed of what our lives would have turned out like if we had ended up together. He will always be a tucked- away dream I keep close to me. I am changed because of him and the love we shared. Can you believe we never even got to kiss? Nope, just a distant love that was breathtaking, and spiritually connected- truly the best, most- treasured love I have ever known, with the least physical contact.

A fairytale love the almost came true. I love you, Kaleb, forever and ever! Thank you for this unforgettable, legendary kind of love- a true love from above! Maybe I'll see you again, and we can share that long- awaited kiss. Maybe in this life, but if not, definitely in the next. We never know the reasons for the seasons of life or love, but you are forever in my heart and you will always be my one and only.

                   I LOVE YOU ALWAYS, KALEB!

Bernadette Padgett
2001/Drug Rehabilitation
September 10, 2001

Suicide Attempt

I had been home from New Life rehab in California for several months now. I remember being severely depressed. I was still adjusting to my bipolar medication and moved back in with my mother and brother. I felt so lost and alone because my entire recovery support system was now in California. I was back home in Arizona because I couldn't find a place to live after rehab. I wanted so badly to stay in Cali with my new found friends, but I just didn't have the financial means.

I felt so out of place, and while I tried to piece my life together and find work, in reality, I was stuck in a rut. All I had left in Arizona was my friends who used drugs. I did my best to stay away from them and, attend 12-step meetings, but I missed the relationships I had built in California in recovery- not to mention Kaleb, who I missed the most! I wanted to pick up where Kaleb and I had left off, and I didn't think I'd ever fall in love like that again!

I was estranged from my mom and brother, and I mostly just stayed home, isolated and depressed. I remember one night in particular, I was in a manic episode. I was terrified and lost and severely suicidal! I remember locking myself in my mom's bedroom and grabbing a belt to try to wrap around my neck and attach it to the closet bar where the clothes hung from. I chickened out, though. I had already been using heroin again, and I had done some earlier that day.

I couldn't handle what I was feeling, and it was like my mother and brother were just oblivious to the pain I was in. People who I thought cared about me, often friends and family have had a pattern of turning a blind eye to my pain. It wasn't anything new to me.

purpose driven/ free to be unapologetically me

2001/Drug Rehabilitation
September 10, 2001
(Suicide Attempt/Cont'd)

I had all I could take that day, and maybe they took notice but just didn't care enough to try to comfort me. I was completely hopeless

I walked up to the nearby gas station and I bought several boxes of pain relievers. I was sobbing, and I'll never forget the clerk asking me if I was ok. I was honest and told him no, and that I wanted to take my life! He did his best to talk me out of it and confided in me that he too attempted suicide at one point in his life. He told me how terrible his experience was and not to do it!

I just put my head down and continued on with my purchase. I walked back to my mom's apartment and locked myself in her bedroom. I downed the bottle of pills and I sat there feeling completely done with life at only 21! I remember I started to fade out and began throwing up. Finally, my mom and brother came and pounded down the door, and called 911.

I was escorted to the hospital by ambulance, but I don't remember the ambulance ride, because by that time, I was unconscious. I remember, at one point, when I was in the hospital in critical condition, the doctor telling my mom he didn't think I was going to make it, and that my organs were shutting down. They forced me to drink some kind of charcoal mix, and hours later, I was admitted to the hospital on suicide watch.

I spent several weeks in the hospital, mostly just sleeping. I kept the blinds closed because I didn't want to face the world. One of the nurses who were assigned to keep an eye on me was so kind and would sit by my bedside and read the Bible to me. She would always open the blinds to let the light shine in. She was like an angel watching over me.

Bernadette Padgett
2001/Drug Rehabilitation
(Suicide Attempt /Cont'd)

My mom and brother visited me time to time, but I just had no idea what I was going to do with my life!

My good friend Heath from California let me stay with him for a short time because I had been using back home in Arizona. He was afraid for me, and wanted to help me out. When I returned home from New Life rehab, he mentioned a lady named Romy who he wanted to introduce me to. He told her about me, and she expressed interest in helping me and wanted to be my sponsor.

It wasn't long after I was released from the hospital after my suicide attempt that I returned to California to FLC (a new rehab facility) after temporarily staying with Heath. Romy did end up becoming my sponsor, and I started my journey of recovery from drug addiction for the second time.

3

Narrative for 2002
(Rehab Again- FLC)

After I had been using again and attempted suicide-, my mother realized I was in a very dangerous place in my life. She paid out of pocket for New Life, and it wasn't cheap. Now, with no money left for rehab, my only choice was to return to California to a state- funded rehabilitation center.

I spoke to Romy just before heading back to California, and she agreed to sponsor me. I was scared and vulnerable, but I knew I needed help! Upon arriving at FLC, I was very frightened! The rehab center was very rundown, and certainly was not a five star rehabilitation center like New Life. I remember calling my mom on the phone, begging her to let me come home, but my mother knew if I did, I would surely use again.

Speaking to the house manager, who wasn't very nice to me, she basically judged me as being 'stuck up.' It wasn't that- I just wasn't used to being in such a rundown facility. I went through a lot at FLC. I ended up traumatized about a quarter of the way through because at exactly 30 days after detox from the heroin and other drugs I had a manic episode. I hadn't been on my bipolar meds while I was using again back home in AZ, so when the drugs were finally completely out of my system, my bipolar disorder surfaced drastically!

Here I was, all alone in rehab, surrounded by strangers and far from my family, and I was out of my mind! I didn't know who I was, or where I was, and I feared for my life! The residents didn't make it any better; in fact, they played into my illness and frightened me even more!

purpose driven/ free to be unapologetically me

Prior to my episode, they would always tell me I looked like a porcelain doll, so when I had my mental break down, part of the way they traumatized me was by saying things like how they liked to play with "dolls" and rip their heads, legs, and arms off! What they did was very uncalled for, and it was their intent to put fear in me!

This type of behavior from the residents went on while I was in the process of, once again, trying new medications to treat my illness. I was often in an episode during the process. At one point, management had me sent to a mental hospital, handcuffed by police, which only terrified me even more and was an unnecessary way of handling the situation!

Right before the police were called, I ran from the facility, and the managers had to chase me down the street and bring me back! They did not call my mother right away. She found out because, while this particular episode was taking place, I happened to be in the kitchen where the phone was located while I was being yelled at by one of the house managers.

My mom called at that very moment, and I answered the phone! My family is very gifted and always knows when something isn't right, even when they're hundreds of miles away!

My mother had me put the house manager on the phone and explained to her I was in a manic episode and to get me to the hospital! I remember my mom telling me just before I handed the phone over to the house manager that she was getting on a plane and would be there within a couple hours!

When I arrived at the hospital after being escorted by police, I was so scared! It's crazy how the mind works, how a person can experience such a thing and still remember the thoughts they had and everything that took place!

Bernadette Padgett

My mother stayed with me in the hospital, sitting by my bedside reading the Bible to me and stayed until they made her leave. But she would return the next morning.

It took about three weeks for the medication to fully take effect and bring me back around. When I was stable again, I was forced to return to FLC. I didn't want to go back and tried to explain what was happening there and how they messed with my mind. But at this point, my mother was so scared if she brought me home, I'd just end up back on heroin, so she had me finish my time at FLC.

About six months later, I completed the program and was able to return home to AZ. I managed to stay sober, but at this point with the mental episode and the entire trauma I experienced while I was at FLC, it took years for me to get back to normal living! There were a lot more instances, like the ripping off the heads, legs, and arms of the "dolls," intended to frighten me that took place. I was in for the long haul to recover from such a traumatic experience!

Once home I lived a very isolated life. I couldn't leave the house without my mother, and didn't want to be alone. My mother had me set up with a new psychiatrist where I continued to be prescribed my bipolar medication. The side effects eventually lead to another problem for me, obesity, which caused more depression.

From what I've learned, most of the medicines to treat bipolar disorder have a side effect of weight gain, because metabolic changes happen, such as the slowing down of metabolism and increased appetite.

For the next several years, I was not only battling mental illness, but also obesity. The following poems reflect my time and experiences at FLC. It was also during that time when I lost my sponsor, Romy. She relapsed and unfortunately didn't make it.

purpose driven/ free to be unapologetically me

2002/ Rehab Again (FLC)
Facing my insanity

Self-Discovery

I know this is just the start of my recovery
And understanding the real me
Is only part of my discoveries
In the light of God's grace
He's put me in this place
To get back to the basics
So I don't continue on with the
Same mistakes
I believe in God's love for the world
Especially when you
Know you are a miracle!
I'm faced with challenges every single day
And when the devil tries
To tempt me
He's only trying to get me to throw my
Life away!
So keeping this reality in mind
I'm keeping God's love for me forever
Until the end of time
Taking it one baby step at a time
Because what God has
In store for me
I know is going to blow my mind!

Bernadette Padgett
2002/ Rehab Again (FLC)

To My Sponsor Romy

Dear Romy,

You are so beautiful, and I know you know you are a miracle! I don't know how to express to you how much I admire you and your courage to be strong! I want you to know you are in my prayers and just remember to keep on keeping on!

Love,
Bernadette

This was written in 2002 when I was in rehab again, at FLC. In 2004 I learned from a dear mutual friend, Heath that she had passed away. She was a true warrior but just not strong enough to beat her disease of addiction. She stood by me as my sponsor, often advocating for me through my trials of my bi-polar disorder surfacing again while in this rehab and the entire trauma I faced while I was there. She was bold and supportive and so loving. I will miss her dearly.

R.I.P my sweet sponsor Romy.

Misery

Misery that courses through my veins
Why must I endure so much pain?
Shame that puts me next to nothing good
Demons and angels that walk
This Earth
Lord, please say I have not been given a curse
The sadness that fills me from
Time to time
Always makes me want to cry
But I promise this time I won't give up the fight
Attitudes that come from deep inside
Can either bury us?
Or
Make us feel so alive!

Bernadette Padgett
2002/ Rehab Again
(FLC)

The Play

Sometimes I feel like I'm in a play
There's a director and He's
Given me lines
To obey
There are days when I feel like I'm enslaved
But no matter the struggle
I know the director is just about to turn the page
And keep me on my way!
These are the simple days of my life
And I see myself through
So many different eyes
Tears of joy and tears of sorrow
Can always make better tomorrows!
So no matter the page my life is on
I must keep on and remember
How in the world did
We get to be so clever?
Life can be so amazing if you just take the time
To try
Be hopeful, loving, and courageous
And always remember…
The director keeps track of the time!

purpose driven/ free to be unapologetically me

2002/ Rehab Again
(FLC)

Hope

Hope is the feeling that seems
To tickle me inside
When I'm feeling like I sometimes want to die
Then I realize that won't work
So I must do what's in
Front of me
So I won't feel so much hurt
When I start to get out of myself
Is when the hope comes on strong
Because this is the point
I realize
I, too, will always and do belong!

Bernadette Padgett
2002/ Rehab Again
(FLC)

Daydreaming

Rainbows in the midnight hour
Don't you know God has that power?
Wishing on a star
That seems to be so far
Only to see the twinkle in your eye
That makes me want to cry
Because I realize how
Quickly life can pass me by
Holding onto each moment so I don't
Blow it
Heavenly angels that will never
Let me down
And knowing this, I get to feel so profound
Looking into a crystal
Let's me know I'm a miracle
And seeing all the prisms of color
Makes me wonder…
How did I stay laid down in that
Misery I was under?
Hearing the laughter of a child's voice
Tells me I now have a choice
Today my life
Is no longer a game!
I have paid the price, and now I choose
Life!

purpose driven/ free to be unapologetically me

2002/ Rehab Again
(FLC)

Heroin

Remembering the day
When you stole my life away
God, how I feel so ashamed!
Anger that musters from all of these insane
Clusters in my mind
Telling me one more time won't hurt
All the while, inside I'm suffering
Fear of a life that is so unknown
Will I be happy? Or be left to fight this terrible
Battle all alone?
Insanity in me, all I do is wreak havoc all around me!
I want to be sane, but I feel so ashamed!
I remember when I took my first shot
I could barely see, let alone walk
All I knew is I needed to throw up
Didn't realize I was doomed from the start and that this would
now be my addictive crutch
It was a love-hate relationship right from the start
A numbing it gave me but with terror it haunted me
A slave to the game, a life of tremendous suffering and pain
Wake up sick, need a fix
Call up the dealer be there in five min
So many I've lost and I was almost one
CPR saved me when I could no longer breathe
No life this was at only 90 pounds my skin so gray
No sign of life in my eyes I was a walking tragedy
What was happening to me I did not know
All the while the drug took over and I was losing my soul at
only 17 years old! Selling my belongings to chase that fix
This was nothing more than a death wish!

Bernadette Padgett
2002/ Rehab Again
(FLC)

Life's Lessons (Part I)

Confinement that's making me wants to scream!
Why does this have to be
The way to get clean?
Sorrows, and anxiety; please help me to get back into
Society
Lives and stories to be told,
The world to me is so unknown
Patience and feelings of despair…
Don't you know how much
I care?!
Time that only ticks minute-by-minute
It's tough when you're
Deep down in it!
God help me to sit through this
And not give up!
On a mission and I'm here to stay
Trying so hard to be brave!
My disease says to leave
But I know in my heart I must hit my knees
If recovery were easy there'd be no struggle
It's real, raw, and it will
Make you humble
To the drawing board I return
I'm the clay in the potter's hand
God rewrite my story
So I may give you the Glory!
Use my story to lift the broken because
I only survived this torment to

purpose driven/ free to be unapologetically me

2002/ Rehab Again
(FLC)

Life's Lessons (Part II)

Fulfill your purpose
Peace I want to share and remember to
Hang in there and not despair!
Let my sorrow be the reason
A life is spared the torment of addiction
Let my story be a lesson
The disease of addiction will affect your entire life!
Hold onto the love inside!
Don't let society pressure you!
Misery loves company
So rise above
Embrace your own self love
Forget needing to fit in
Be your own person!
And spare yourself the heartache
I made my mistakes
But I'm making up for it by leading others to faith
Through God's saving Grace
This is my sole purpose
I now know what my worth is!

Bernadette Padgett
2000-2002/ Rehab Again
(New Life/FLC)

The following notes are from my dearest best friend Rayna, who has passed away, and my friend Jeff, who I met in 12-step recovery back home in Arizona. Both notes are very special to me from these two friends. I've had them with me for 20 years now!

I cherish the love I shared with these friends among many more who have been with me during my struggles of addiction and my path to recovery.

Rayna was one of the sweetest, most loving people I had ever met! She and I were so much alike, and even into our 20s, we both were still very much like little girls inside. We both loved to write and often carried our pretty journals with us wherever we went. She was more like a sister to me, and I miss her every day! A beautiful soul she was, and her heart is with me forever! She is my guardian angel who I know watches over me and my daughter! I love you always, Miss Rayna!

purpose driven/ free to be unapologetically me

Burnie,   Feb 14,00

When I move to ACA, New Mexico I'll miss you so much but I'll be okay because I have faith that you'll do great. Well I'm away, I want you to be happy! I'm going to be so lonley & I'll realy miss you so much! When I finaly get home though we'll both be healthy & happy.

I love you

Rayna Marie
Andrews

Happy Valentines day!

You are Beautiful Valentine

Love Rayna

12-1-01 Bernadette

Hi its me you beautiful friend Rayna Marie, Your sitting right next to me & my silly Goose is in the bathroom. I don't want you to go to California however you deserve to get clean so I will be happy for you! You truly are a friend & you'll always be in my heart.

Yours forever,
Rayna

purpose driven/ free to be unapologetically me

BERNADETTE

THANK YOU FOR THE PLEASURE OF ALLOWING ME TO BASQUE IN THE RADIANCE OF YOUR BEAUTY. WITHOUT YOU I AM NOTHING. WITH YOU, I AM EVERYTHING.

I CAN ONLY SAY THAT I AM A BETTER PERSON FOR HAVING MET YOU. A PLACE IN MY HEART YOU SHALL FOREVER HOLD.

JEDI.

Bernadette Padgett

Me 21 Years Old/ Rehab at New Life 2001

4

Narrative for 2002-2005
(Isolation)

I spoke of returning home to AZ after my second rehabilitation at FLC and how the medication I was on to treat my bipolar disorder caused me to become obese. It was during this time I lost my identity. I didn't even recognize myself in the mirror, and I certainly didn't like what I saw. I was ashamed of myself and my body, and I chose to isolate because I was terrified of anyone I once knew seeing me like that!

I tried to work part- time here and there, but the depression and the way I would get made fun of going out into the world was more than I could take. I found myself just wanting to hide behind closed doors. I was unmotivated to do anything about it at the time, and I sunk deeper and deeper into the pits of despair. I remember just wanting and needing to be held so badly, wanting someone who would just love and accept me the way I was, big and all. My soul was aching and I needed love.

I had no friends at this point in my life- partly by choice because I just couldn't face anyone with the way I looked and felt about myself. I felt like an utter failure. I wanted nothing more but to hide away. So that is exactly what I did for quite some time.

The following poems reflect my isolation period and what I was feeling and longing for…

purpose driven/ free to be unapologetically me

2002-2005/ Isolation

Crowd-Fearing

There's a large crowd of people
It's scary because I don't feel like an equal
I spot you from a distance
You're glowing and laughing
With such charisma
As I draw closer my stomach
Begins to turn
I chicken out, and into the corner I return
This isolation game is driving me
Insane!
Alone is not where I want to be
Because then all I'd say is poor me
I do not want to live in
Self-pity!
There is nothing beautiful about it!
A cloud is over my head
And the distance in my heart is
Making me want to flee
But there you are and you approach me
You pull me up by my arm
When our eyes meet once again
I realize without a doubt I have a
True friend!

Bernadette Padgett
2002-2005/Isolation

Putting It In To Perspective

Anti-social/Socialite
The way she perceives herself
She's afraid of crowds, but she wants to
Stand out
She's a quiet thing, and she's
Learning how to
Live clean
Don't be so concerned with friends
Because I've got plenty
In the heavens!
Your dreams of dancing, writing,
And making yourself known
Is all there waiting for you
I'm meant to be someone and I'm choosing
To live this life to the
Fullest!
I'm gaining confidence every
Single day
Because a life of abundance is
Why God pulled me
Out of the grave!
I am the only one that can stop me
From this incredible gift of life
I've decided to use my talents
And give this thing a try!
A lifetime of lessons, I've got plenty
Of encouragement to give

purpose driven/ free to be unapologetically me   2002-2005/Isolation
(Longing for Love)

Searching for the Love of My Life
Romance is all I want
Can't you see that my insides are all torn up?
This feeling of emptiness, and loneliness
Is making me into such a mess!
This is when I should be acting my best!
I worry about how I dress
Because I want to be seen in a state of
Beauty and completeness
Where is my knight in shining armor?
I wonder if the fantasy
I ponder
Will ever come true, in this life I must wander?
I feel such sorrow when I see
Love being shared
Because I fear I will always be on the outside
Looking in
Watching the love shared
Instead of being the one about whom someone cares
How can I turn my fears around?
I don't want to continue
In a life of despair!
If there is someone out there for me
I pray he finds me
And loves me just the way I am!
That we become best friends
And love one another
Like only true love can!
Turning tragedy into triumph is where
I think I'll begin

5

Narrative for 2002-2005/ Mental Affliction
(Bipolar disorder/drug addiction)

The following poems describe my desire to escape my mental insanity, feelings of being trapped, and just wanting to be free of it all. I also reflect on what happened to me as a teenager in 1995 when I overdosed on LSD, as briefly mentioned in the previous narrative for 2001.

I was only 15 years old when a group of friends from high school began experimenting with the drug. We all got together at Avery's parents' house to drop acid. I, being the dare devil I was, decided to take 3 tabs at once! I didn't realize the effect and was unaware of how strong this particular LSD was. Come to find out later, the person I had bought it from triple- dipped the tabs, and I was actually tripping on nine hits- not three!

The trip started normally. I was, laughing, seeing tracers, breathing walls, hearing colors, and feeling music very vividly! Soon though, it turned into a bad trip, and I had unknowingly opened what seemed to be a door to another dimension.

The spiritual aspect took effect and went from moments of heaven to hell. It went on for hours until eventually my friends called my mom, and she picked me up and took me straight to the hospital. God saved me through this, and I will never forget what I saw and experienced! What good it did was make me never doubt the existence of God! I use my experience to warn others of the dangers of LSD in hopes they will take my word for it and never have to go down the path I did!

purpose driven/ free to be unapologetically me

2002-2005/Mental Affliction
(Bipolar disorder)

Pleading with God

Birds in flight, I'm doing alright
I imagine you here
Where our spirits unite
I'm walking a thin line
Reaching for the stars on this journey
I am on
I stare at the clouds in awe
Wishing to be something
I am not
What the heck is going on?
Do you hear me?
I'm in so much agony!
How do I escape? Please give me a break!
I've witnessed your love
And I realize it's from above
Please hold my hand and
Bring me back to peace and serenity
Again, before I'm permanently lost
In this insanity I'm in!
A thought comes to mind…
Am I crazy?
Or have I just run out of time?
I'm trapped within myself
Please God get me out!
Or just bury me
Without any doubt!

Bernadette Padgett
"Wrote in 2002/Took Place 1995"
(Mental Affliction/Drug Addiction)
Spiritual Warfare

The Trip Beyond Normal Existence

Portals and dimensions in time
I've lived through spiritual battle and have experienced
The other side.
If you wonder if demons and angels exist
Let me bear witness I've
Experienced this
I've seen what others may never
In this lifetime!
Tripping on LSD gave me access to
An alternative existence
I will never forget!
Crying out for God to save me
I've seen so much!
These are the things you only read of
But at 15 years old I was
Fighting for my soul
I am so blessed that God never let me go!
I prayed for forgiveness and God took mercy on me
I live to tell the story to give warning
LSD is no joke!
It opens you up to a world unknown
That is always there behind the scenes
Not many will actually get to see
With their own eyes
But for whatever reason I did
I have no doubt my Lord and Savior exists and his love for me!
And those heavenly angels are always watching over me!

purpose driven/ free to be unapologetically me

6

Narrative 2005-2006
(Still Dreaming of Love)

In the next poems, I describe my feelings of longing for love and wanting people around me to see the real me not what's on the outside. I also share the love I still had for Heath and how hard it was for me when I learned he was married.

I was still isolated during this time in my life, and I continued to Miss California and the friends and support when I had lived there when I was first in treatment at New Life. It took a long time for me to let go of missing those friends and my life out there, but eventually I was able to move forward and accept the changes taking place. Even through these times of continuing to dream of love, I always had hope…

purpose driven/ free to be unapologetically me

2005/Still Dreaming of Love

Taking the Blinders Off

"Beauty is in the eye of the beholder"
I think that's how the
Saying goes...
It's what someone chooses to see
Within that others
Don't take the time to know
Outside flaws
Prevent seeing the beauty underneath
It takes a special soul
To look past and truly see me
Without the clouded vision
Of what everyone else only tends to see
That's why many never get to
Know the real me
Shallowness that robs you of love
When deep inside
There's a beautiful treasure waiting if only
They had taken the time
To let me inside
Some will just never know but that's ok
Not everyone is meant to
Experience my loving soul
Only the ones with the beauty to match
Who choose to look past
Those are the special people
Worth letting me know
I can be myself and walk this journey
Knowing whole heartedly who's on my side
And the ones who belong to my
Tribe!

Bernadette Padgett
2005/Still Dreaming of Love

A Special Kind of Love

Love is a special gift that comes
From up above
Especially when you know
You're in love.
I dream of a guy I would like to meet
Someone who would
Sweep me off my feet
Love from afar is a splendid way to share
The feelings I might have
With that special
Kind of care
God only knows who is meant for me
And I shall bask in the light
Of this new and wonderful
Opportunity!

Heath *(Part I)*

With eyes so wide
Looking up to the heavens again,
I think I have found
My friend
A creative type who won't
Give up the fight
If he only knew; if he only knew
The love I have for him
He sparkles like a
Gem
Picture perfect I see us two
A genuine love before
The fame
I see you now face to face and I
Hope you are the same
So bitter sweet
This time to keep
I keep a picture of you close
Along with things
I treasure most
Your eyes so bright looking up
At a starry night
I really do see you
I don't know if you've already
Fallen in love, but I do
Believe you're meant for me
I really hope you are the one!
Careful now for my feelings are tender
I'm the same but better; don't you remember?

Bernadette Padgett
2006/Still Dreaming of Love

Heath (Part II)

Please don't judge me for my size; for what's inside
Is your prize
I escape to my thoughts of you
And I yearn to hold you
Through and through
Be patient
My loved ones say
For this man is gonna stay
Hope you feel the same for me
Because our love
Could grow endlessly
Years down the road, I see you perform
And I learn you fell in love
With a child on the way
That day tore a hole in my heart
And as you kissed me on my head goodbye
A piece of me became dead inside
Oh, how I longed to be
Your wife
I've seen you online and you seem happy
As ever! A beautiful wife and
Daughter
I'm happy you married another!
I set you free
And it's ok you didn't marry me
Just glad to see you're dancing on the wings
Of living out your life long
Dreams! God bless you, Heath!

purpose driven/ free to be unapologetically me

7

Narrative for 2006
(The Relapse)

Around this time, I remember going to visit my aunt and uncle here and there in the East Valley. I wanted to be close to family, and it was very hard being isolated and having negative feelings about being overweight.

I had been dabbling with heroin off and on and was becoming addicted once again. The pain, sorrow, and isolation lead me back to using because it was just too painful for me to bear.

One particular day, I went to stay over at my aunt's house; I was dope sick and went over to rest. I remember my aunt stayed in the living room with me while I lay on the couch, drifting in and out of sleep and feeling the effects of with drawl. She told me later how she kept a close eye on me as my breathing was very suppressed, and she had been praying for me.

The next poem is about my aunt seeing an angel watching over me while she had been praying as I lay there, sick and detoxing from heroin…

purpose driven/ free to be unapologetically me

2006/The Relapse
(Dope Sick)

Awakening

An orange glow in the center
I shall remember this
Forever
Iridescent wings
Bigger than a dream
A beautiful being hovering over me
A mess I was not knowing
This was real
Someone else saw and this
Is what I feel
How can this be?
An angel hovering over me
Protecting me?
Sick and beaten down I was a young soul
Slipping away
All my family could do was pray
Not to worry as unhealthy as
I was, with self-inflicting pain
My angel from above
Had come to me this day
My auntie starring in awe
There was nothing left to say
God had his hand on me and
Sent his angel my way
A feather left in remembrance
You can guarantee this was anything but a dream
I am really blessed and a return from the living dead I will
forever be!

8

Narrative for 2008
(Long Suffering/Waiting on Love)

By this time, I had accepted my weight gain for the most part, and I began to join society again. I had just graduated from medical coding school a year prior, bought a Honda (which I had always wanted), and was finally out on my own again in my own apartment. I also landed a job as a marketing director for an assisted living facility and I was doing very well!

Even still, I was lonely. It had been many years since I dated, and I still didn't feel good about myself because of being overweight. I often let it keep me from doing the things I enjoyed.

I was making some new friends from work and was going back to church. Things were looking up. I just remember the painful nights and how I still longed to be held, loved, and kissed. It had been so long since I was kissed by a man, and it was really starting to weigh on me.

I felt very ostracized from life especially in regards to love and the opposite sex. I told myself I was hideous and that no man would ever want me, let alone date me and, especially marry me.

The following poems reflect the inner pain I was in with this as my reality and the longing for love that I was experiencing…

purpose driven/ free to be unapologetically me

2008/ Long Suffering
(Waiting on Love)

A Letter to Jesus,

I yearn so deeply to feel and be loved, to know what true love really is and what it feels like. It's been so long since I've been touched by a hand that truly loves me. Lord, please reveal to me your perfect, unconditional love. Let me know I'm special too in sweet ways only you can do. Please let me know how to unconditionally love and be loved.

I feel such loneliness and despair in this life. I want so badly to just give up! But something keeps telling me to fight! How do I live this life? What do you want from me, Lord? What's it going to take? I'm ready and, willing; please don't give up on me for Heaven's sake.

When you look deep into my eyes, the pain is so relevant and clear. I shed tear after tear. I try to find peace year after year, but my heart continues to ache. What did I do to deserve this loneliness and pain that seeps through every part of my soul?

Show me your love, Jesus, and help me to make you my first priority. I don't want to make the same mistakes and end up back where I was. Help me to long for you and set my eyes on you first and foremost. Please hold my hand and walk me through this darkness and pain. I seek you and want to feel you with me. Please don't ever leave me!

I've been dealing with a longtime wounded heart, and sometimes the pain is so great, I feel I can't even breathe! I feel set apart from the rest of the world. As I see people come and go, living a life I only dream of, married and with children I ponder my existence. Was I meant to do this all alone?

Bernadette Padgett
2008/ Long Suffering
(Waiting on Love)
"Dear Jesus, Cont'd"

The desire is so great, and the lack in my life is so real; I can't fully put into words how badly I feel. I often wonder why God hasn't allowed me to become a wife.

What is this life all about if you can't experience it with your life partner? As I sit here writing at this coffee shop on a Thursday in April 2008, I ask you, Jesus, to put your hand in mine and walk me through this journey called life.

purpose driven/ free to be unapologetically me

2008/Long Suffering
(Waiting on Love)

Pondering While I Wait

On this day I sit in my living room
And pray
Still with the same inner longings
And heartache
Just trying to wait patiently for my
True love to find me
It's like I'm in a whirlwind
Just keeps circling the same scenario
Eagerly hoping for a
Miracle
How much longer, God, do I have to suffer?
How much longer must I
Live like this?
I don't know what lesson I've missed
But it seems like
When love is near
I just crumble with fear
Will love find me this year?

Bernadette Padgett
2008/Long Suffering
(Waiting on Love)

Yearning

How long can one endure?
Pain that seems to last forevermore?
I've loved and lost; time and time again
Only to repeat the same sadness that lies from deep within
I often wonder what this life is all about?
I can't help but feel my time is
Running out
Yet with the morning light that comes
With each new day
My heart yearns for something wonderful
And magical to come my way
To break up the monotony that comes with
Each passing day
When I long for my soulmate
But never catch that break
A piece of me gets left behind, and
It becomes harder and harder to keep that dream alive
Like missing pieces to the puzzle get
Scattered all around
And the only thing that can put me
Back together
Is the love I have not yet found
As time continues to tick away, so is that voice inside me
struggling to keep
Believing
Or tell myself to just stop dreaming
It's ironic how heavy a heart can get, yet

purpose driven/ free to be unapologetically me

2008/Long Suffering
(Waiting on Love)

Yearning cont'd...

Still continue to beat
I'm afraid of passing before
Anyone gets the chance to get to know the real me
Before I'm presented with
That wonderful opportunity
Though the results are just not up to me
I can't begin to express the hurt of uncertainty
Or how much this dream really
Means to me
But maybe before long
God will finally break up this monotony
Going to choose to be strong
One more time
While I hang onto this dream
I'm struggling
To keep
Alive!

Bernadette Padgett
2008/Long Suffering
(Waiting on Love)

Dear God,

Well, it's already July and soon the year will be over. I pray I will meet someone and fall in love at least before this year comes to an end. I don't think I can bear another winter of loneliness, despair, and dreadful agony. I long for someone to just cuddle up next to me and hold me.

At another coffee shop I sit and write, trying so hard to be lifted up and put a smile on my face. Even though in reality, I'm suffering such painful heartache.

I wish I knew what to do about my aching heart. I can't give up, but I can't even part with the longing for love. I try to think of a way to release the pain, so I set a balloon free with my hopes and dreams. It's not yet time to go, but I have to admit that in my present circumstance, if things don't change, I don't know how life will go, hanging onto a world with such longing in my soul.

I often wonder why I can't just enjoy life without being bogged down with such depression and fear. Will I ever get to live a life without so many tears?

Things have gotten better for me, I must say. But I'm still waiting for the blessing of a full life and to become a wife.

purpose driven/ free to be unapologetically me

9

Narrative for 2008
(Choosing Accountability)

By now I was fed up! It had been far too long that I had been without a boyfriend, and I knew it was up to me to change it! Not that you have to be thin to have a boyfriend, but I wanted to feel good about myself when I was dating and I wanted to love myself, and feel beautiful again, so I could be happy and enjoy the person I was with. I did not want to second guess and ask; will this man love and accept me?

I was at a cross- road, and I knew there was only one way to go! I was prayed up, toughening up, and ready to take the leap! I was determined to get a new lease on life, and this is exactly what I did!

The following vow describes the way in which I motivated myself to make a change, get honest with myself, and take a leap of faith!

purpose driven/ free to be unapologetically me

July 2008/Choosing Accountability

Today I am choosing to take responsibility for my life- my past, present, and future. I am empowered that I have the ability to make healthy, positive choices in my life and reap the good rewards from it.

I choose to be positive, happy, reasonable with myself, and others, and to trust in God. As long as I choose to do my part in what God wants me to do, happiness is sure to follow!

10

Narrative for 2009
(Battling Obesity/Longing for Love Continues…)

   The following is the start of my weight loss journey, why I was doing it, my before picture, and what I experienced in the process.

I was still longing for love on this journey, but even still, I was ready! I started counseling, and I was changing my eating habits, and working out.

My heart was still very heavy while this transformation was taking place, but I did finally realize in this process of the pain is I was finally making a necessary change that would ultimately get me the very thing I always longed for… "Love." Most importantly, it included self- love…

purpose driven/ free to be unapologetically me

2009/Struggling with weight loss
(Battling Obesity)

"My Why"

    Losing weight is tough, but not as tough as I was making it! The happiness that's to come is well- worth the fight! It's a daily struggle- forcing myself to go to the gym, eating healthy, drinking enough water, and not eating late at night, but it's what I need to do for me to be happy within myself!

    I want so much to be able to look in the mirror and like what I see again! Conquering one pound at a time, and already lost ten pounds, which lifted my spirit! I'm looking forward to seeing everyone at Christmas time and be fifty pounds lighter! What joy that will bring!

    I'm so glad I finally made the decision to act and fight the good fight for weight loss! I know good things are on the way, I literally can't wait! God help me to be patient with my progress and stay out of your way! I trust you're working behind the scenes, making this journey everything I hope and pray it will be! With hard work and dedication, I will be in the skin I want to be in, flying high on the wings of life! No more settling or giving up! Embracing this life given to me by making the decision to get and be healthy!

Bernadette Padgett
2009/Struggling with weight loss
(Battling Obesity)

Before

purpose driven/ free to be unapologetically me

2009/Struggling with weight loss
(Battling Obesity)

This is me at 262 pounds! I hate my body, I hate that I can't even breathe! But most of all, I hate me!

People look at me and stare, they laugh and say, "Look how fat that girl is over there!" Even though I am so big, no one sees me. The biggest girl in the room, but the most invisible!

Do you see me? I am the invisibly obese. What a struggle this has been; I took medication to fight the depression and this is what it did! I stand alone with the odds against me, suicide becoming more and more appealing.

Is there a way out? I want to believe there's a better life out there waiting for me! Is it too late? Can't take any more heartbreak or heartache!

Bernadette Padgett
2009/The Longing for Love Continues

A Perfect Love is Worth the Wait

Let your beautiful wings encompass my life, so that
I may soar to the highest of highs
A place where the thought of pain is merely
A memory
And those perfect sunset hours
On the sand, is where I
Plan to be
Where we will be hand in hand
In perfect harmony
Blessed with the seed God planted
In my heart,
I only had to water it, and now we're never
Apart
I longed many years for you, but
The thought kept fading away
Doubt in my mind is how I ended each and
Every day
But a tiny voice kept saying, wait and pray
That is when you found me
A dream comes true!
Just like a lost soul strolling in the rain
The picture is gloom and seems a dreary end
But that's when God does
The unexpected and
When I found my best friend!

purpose driven/ free to be unapologetically me

2009/The Longing for Love Continues

Window Pain

As I peer out the window and watch the cars
Pass me by
There's nothing left but a deep
Hole in my heart
And no more room to cry
Faith really is a mystery and as the days
Get shorter my agony
Multiplies
The dreaded lonely nights
I'm growing weary and I can't accept the pain
It's hard to see life
Worth living without someone to love
I look up above, but still I sit waiting
To fall in love

Bernadette Padgett
2009/The Longing for Love Continues
(Despair)

Symphony of Pain

I'm child-like and afraid
I can't look back
There's nowhere to escape
I walk this journey
alone
Broken, hurting, lonely
With nowhere left to go
If sadness were a symphony, the melody
Could be without an end
A haunting sound of darkness that settles in
All the while I long and wish for God to bring me
My husband
Can I endure all of this until the bitter end?

purpose driven/ free to be unapologetically me

11

Narrative for 2011-Jan. 2013
(Weight Loss Journey Continues/Battling Obesity)

The following describe my continued weight loss journey, the steps I was taking, the way I motivated myself, and ultimately, what worked for me-, including my success story!

I hope my experience opens the reader's eyes to know if you are going through a similar journey with weight loss, you can do it too! Dreams do not have to be out of reach!

Throughout my experience and the choices I've made, I remembered to include Jesus because it was He who gave me the strength!

purpose driven/ free to be unapologetically me

2011/Weight loss Journey Continues
(Battling Obesity)

***My Goal:**

Starting today, January 18th, 2011, my current weight is 182 pounds. I've lost 80 pounds so far! My goal is to lose 30 pounds by March 31st, 2011! That is 10 weeks from now, which will make my weight 152 pounds!

To achieve this, I must continue to walk at least 40 minutes every day, make sure I eat a healthy breakfast, lunch, and dinner, and try to eat every three hours. If I need a snack, I need to make it a healthy choice. No eating out until March 31st! Don't eat past 7 pm and pack my food to go when I'm not at home.

With the 80 pounds I've already lost- and only 30 pounds to go- I know I can do this! I'm making a difference in my life starting today!

I claim a new lease on life, and I'm nearing the finish line!
God, I know anything is achievable, and I draw strength, self-control, self-discipline, and perseverance from you, Lord!

May I achieve my goal and be an inspiration to those who struggle with obesity and depression.

Bernadette Padgett
Jan 2012/Weight loss Journey Continues
(Battling Obesity)

Dear God,

I am in complete defeat over my binge eating! I am completely powerless over this food addiction! I emotionally over ate today so bad! I feel so out of control! I'm already back in the 200 pound mark! I don't know what happened. I was doing so well! I was all the way down to 175 pounds! I'm miserable, and I don't know how to consistently change! Please help me to stop this insanity!

I want to be thin again and happy! I feel hopeless every time I try something new, and I mess up on my diet and lack of exercise. I'm scared of the direction I'm headed. Please help me to turn it around. I can't do it without you! Please give me what I need to get through this and reach my goal by my birthday.

I don't want to live a life of fear, isolation, misery, and depression! I want to be happy, confident, beautiful, and attract the man of my dreams! Please help me to take it meal by meal, workout by workout, day by day, and not forget to pray, pray, pray! Help me to get through each day successfully by making a dent in my weight loss a little at a time, pound by pound. Help me to not give up, but persevere no matter what!

I'm turning this desire over to you. Give me strength to do what I have to do for my happiness and ability to love myself! With you my dreams will come to pass, and I know my weight loss will last!

purpose driven/ free to be unapologetically me

February 2012/Weight loss Journey Continues
(Battling Obesity)

Today was a good day! I ate healthy and walked 40 minutes ya ya! I even downloaded a fitness app that tracks my calories, food intake, and exercise. It helps me stay on track and calculate my goals. I'm getting closer to my goal weight every day, and I know as long as I stay on track and continuously work at it I will reach my weight loss goal of 100 pounds! I'm so excited I made the decision to do this! I'll be looking like myself again in no time!

I look forward to treating myself to a new wardrobe from my favorite clothing website that has all the rockabilly pinup fashion trends! Love me some Old Hollywood fashion!

I may even go visit some old friends from California because I know they'd be happy for me to see how far I've come! Just for today I've succeeded at getting closer to my goal! I feel happy, joyous, and free! Looking forward to the new skinny me!

I have finally made the decision that I love myself enough to complete my goal. I have gone through a long waiting period for my dreams to unfold. I realize it's not in my time, but always on time, and in God's time!

Bernadette Padgett
November 2012/Weight loss Journey Continues
(Battling Obesity)

Weight Loss Motivation/Affirmations
(What worked for me)

1. Do not obsessively weigh, or inspect yourself in the mirror, hoping to look thinner.

2. Do workout without setting rules on how long, or how much exercise to do; just do something every day.

3. Make two healthy meal choices daily. (Try to limit soda, sweets, and junk food.) *Limit eating out.*

4. Eat healthy carbohydrates early in the day.

5. Prepare for success ahead of time, by preparing healthy snacks to go.

6. Be mindful; think about what you want and plan to eat and what the results will be beforehand to determine if this will help you achieve weight loss or add weight.
(In doing so, you can focus on how making healthy food choices will bring you closer to your desired weight)

7. Stop making excuses! Don't limit whether you will get your workout in based on the weather, wanting to get ready for the day and do my hair and makeup, or what I feel like wearing instead of my gym clothes.

purpose driven/ free to be unapologetically me

November 2012/Weight loss Journey Continues
(Battling Obesity)

Weight Loss Motivation/Affirmations
(What worked for me)

Note to Self:

* Every time I make an excuse to do the opposite of what will get me to my desired weight and body image, I am sabotaging and robbing myself by, and taking away a piece of my happiness, good breaks, miracles, and of having a fulfilling, healthy life. I am taking away my chances for my divine appointment with my future husband that can come within a blink of an eye, just by being in the right place at the right time.

* I must prepare myself for this and get ready for those blessings because I want to present the best, healthiest version of myself so I may wholeheartedly receive what God is giving me in my life.

* I know and believe I am worthy of the blessing of true love because I am being true to myself and love myself enough to transform, inside and out!

* Beauty comes from within, so when I eat healthy, I receive the proper nutrition to look and feel better!

* When I exercise I am getting rid of toxins, and extra un-wanted fat. It cleans out my pores, and sheds weight, which ultimately will lead to a "better me" all the way around.

* Getting in shape is not just for "looks" or to feel better, but to also bring better relationships into my life with my friends and family, to have a more fulfilling and busy social life without the need to break plans or isolate myself.

Bernadette Padgett
Jan 2013/Weight loss Journey Cont'd/ New Year!

Positive Mindset

1. The dreams and my heart's desires I hope for are attainable.

2. It starts with "Me" one healthy food choice at a time, exercise, and a positive state of mind!

3. Keeping busy in between and staying physically active will ignite my dreams into a living reality!

4. Exercise doesn't have to feel like work! Do what you love that requires movement and you'll enjoy it and have fun while you're doing it!

5. For every 10 pounds I lose, treat myself to a non-food reward!

<u>Daily Goals</u>
1. Every morning, get on my knees and pray in faith and gratitude. And include others in my prayers.
2. Read the Bible and daily devotionals.
3. Make one meal a day a green smoothie or protein shake.
4. Take my vitamins and drink only sugar- free drinks.
Keep up with my water intake.
5. Make wise, healthy food choices, and if possible, plan my meals a day in advance.
6. Thirty minutes of physical activity daily.
7. Make time for quiet time to reflect over the day, meditate, be mindful and present in the moment, and to become more self-aware and aware of the needs of others.
8. Write down what I'm thankful for that day, and take a daily inventory to correct my wrongs and strive to do better the next
9. Speak only words of love, positivity, and kindness over myself and others, and the direction my life is going.
10. Continue to set attainable goals and work towards them, and give myself credit not just for the milestone in which I succeeded, but also the journey along the way. Stay grateful!

January 2013/Weight loss Journey Continues
(Battling Obesity)

After
Lost 100 pounds!

 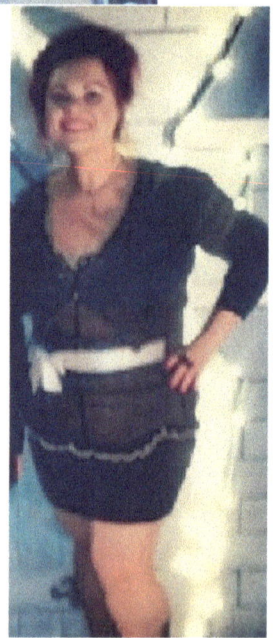

Bernadette Padgett
January, 2013/Weight loss Journey Continues
(Battling Obesity)

This is me; I lost 100 pounds! No way is medication or this cruel and shallow world gonna bring me down!

I love my life, but most importantly, I love myself! I don't care anymore if anyone sees me. I am finally free and back to being me!

Believe in yourself and follow your dreams, and you can overcome and achieve anything! God has more in store for me than I can ever dream. No matter what this life brings, I believe it is worth the fight! I won't give up! Not on this life!

Thank you to those who supported me along the way, in my heart, you will forever stay! And Gamma M. G., thank you for pushing me through! Always encouraging me to get to the gym and eat healthy! You made me happy and made my weight loss journey bearable! So happy for my transformation! God really does work miracles!

purpose driven/ free to be unapologetically me

12

Narrative for March 2013
(Overcoming Life's Challenges)

The following is all about my strength and determination to overcome life's obstacles! How I continued to pray through the process of life, and have hope through it all…

March 2013/Overcoming Life's Challenges

Reality Check

Today is a good day! No matter the heartache, disappointments, or setbacks. God is good and He loves me. No matter who has failed me, they are not in control of my blessings or my destiny. God promises to restore and repay everything that has been stolen from me.

All the years I've lost, God will make up for it in abundance so that the years to come will be better than the years past! I'm making great strides, and breakthrough is just on the horizon. My dreams are coming to pass!

God will never leave me. He created me with the dreams in my heart, and He will make a way when it seems there isn't one. I have overcome obstacles many would not be able to accomplish all because I chose faith and to rely upon God.

I know the Lord is going to take me further, faster in the coming weeks than I ever dreamed possible. I must get up every day with an attitude of faith, regardless of my pain.

God is paying me back with His goodness and favor for everyone in my life who has wronged and abandoned me. Maybe one day, they will seek me out to make right their wrongs. That's really not up to me, but I have forgiven those who have hurt me and set myself free. I trust in my Lord and Savior for the battle is not mine, but His.

I choose to trust in him for the amazing turn- around and transformation happening in my life. Surely, goodness and mercy shall follow me all the days of my life. I know I can expect great things and miracles to come, for the Lord knows what I've endured, years of pain, sorrow, sadness, loneliness, and long suffering. I am claiming a flood of God's goodness and blessings. I need not worry or fret.

Bernadette Padgett
March 2013/Overcoming Life's Challenges
(Reality Check/ Cont'd)

It's not up to me to figure out the when or the how, but to just trust his perfect timing! I trust I will be in amazement and witness the Lord's beautiful promises taking place in my life. I love you, Father, and peace I send out to my friends and family.

Today I Declare

1. I am beautiful.

2. I am able.

3. I am healed.

4. I am strong.

5. I have many talents.

6. The world needs me.

7. I am loved.

8. I am whole.

9. I am at peace.

10. I am experiencing breakthroughs and God's promises are coming true for me.

11. I have wisdom beyond my time.

12. I am special and courageous.

13. I have a lot to offer.

14. I am insightful.

15. I am creative, unique, and inventive

purpose driven/ free to be unapologetically me

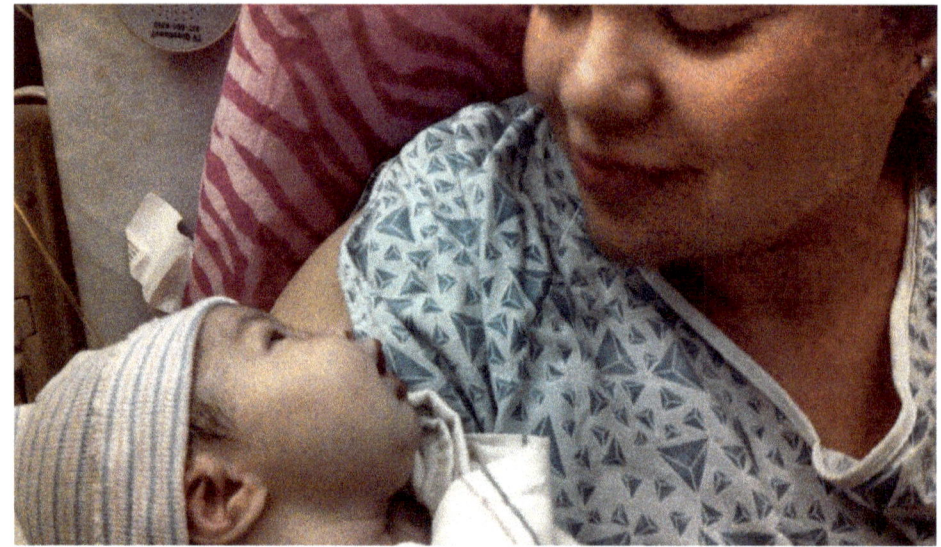

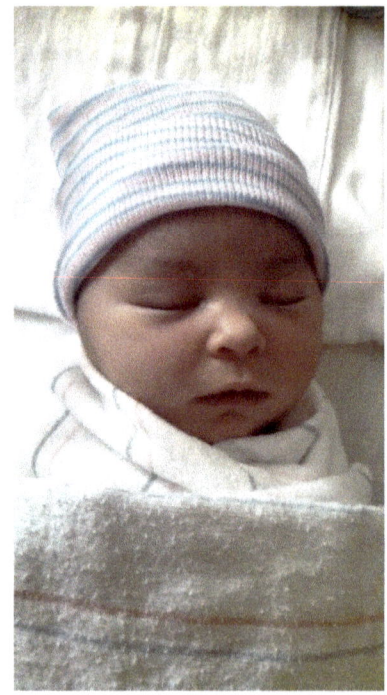

It's A Girl!

13

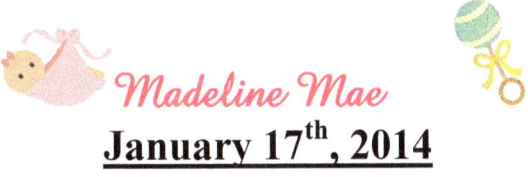

January 17th, 2014
Narrative for Life Event
(Birth of My Daughter Madeline)

I met my daughter's father when I was living at an apartment in Peoria, AZ sometime around 2012. He worked for a carpet cleaning company and apparently we met a year prior to that when I had my carpets cleaned.

I was sitting outside on my porch and he noticed me and reminded me that we had met a year prior. He told me I was cute. We exchanged numbers, but I didn't call him until about three days later. We were only dating for a couple months when he told me he was already in a relationship and was going back to her.

I was completely heartbroken, but I was able to move forward with my life. About four months had passed and one day out of the blue, he showed up at my apartment and said he was leaving his current relationship and wanted me back. I had been single for quite some time before Devin and I met, and I was lonely and in need of love and affection, so I decided to go for it!

He moved in with me fairly quickly. He was recovering from a car accident and couldn't work at the time, so I took on the financial responsibilities. A month or so into the relationship, I noticed his behavior towards me included some verbal abuse, insults, and disrespect. I wasn't happy, and I decided to leave him because I felt I deserved to be treated better. Devin went back to his ex and moved out.

I ended communication with him and I didn't want any contact, so I decided to move once again to Scottsdale.

I remember it had been four months and I was having morning sickness and just wasn't feeling like myself. I took a pregnancy test and it came up negative. I figured it was accurate and didn't think twice about it. I did notice I was gaining weight, even though I was still working out from time to time.

There was a morning in particular I awoke from a dream I will never forget! I dreamed I was living in a house on a corner street and a little girl with long dark hair and I were playing hula hoop outside in the front lawn. She was chasing me and calling me mama and I told her, "Honey I'm not your mama," but the little girl kept chasing me saying, "Mama! Mama!" and laughing and having fun!

The dream was so real that the next day, I told my mom about it. I didn't know until later that she had been observing me and my morning sickness so she decided to take me to the doctor for an ultrasound and pregnancy test. And sure enough, I was pregnant!

The ultrasound showed I was four months pregnant! I was so overwhelmed with the news that I began to cry because here I was 33 years old and single, and I didn't want to raise my child alone. My mother and I talked and she agreed she would help me raise my child so I decided to keep her.

My pregnancy went fairly well. However, while under the care of my OBGYN towards the end of my pregnancy, I noticed I was having some breathing problems. Come to find out after giving birth to my daughter, I apparently had a UTI for which my doctor never treated me. Because it went un-treated, it turned into a very bad case of pneumonia and then A.R.D.S. (acute respiratory distress syndrome).

I became septic just days after delivering my baby and ended up in the I.C.U., intubated on a vent and fighting for my life!

Bernadette Padgett

I was still bleeding as well from just giving birth! My poor new born baby girl was being passed around my friends' and family's' houses while I was dying in the hospital. My mom refused to leave my side, and we didn't want to have my new born staying in the hospital with a chance of getting sick. It was a horrible time, one which should have been the happiest!

I'll never forget just before they put me on the vent; I was feeling like death was approaching me, and I was terrified and looked over to my mother, and in a whisper said. "Do I need to say my goodbyes?" She exclaimed "NO!" "We walked into this hospital together, and we're walking out together!" That's the last I remember until about 10 days later when I was finally coming off the vent and regaining consciousness.

If anyone is unfamiliar with A.R.D.S it usually occurs when someone is in a car accident and their lungs are severely injured bleed. They can no longer inflate to receive oxygen. In my case, it was a result of an untreated infection.

I remember when I came to I thought I had dreamed of having a baby, but I was assured it was not a dream. I had a long road to recovery, and I had to be on a BIPAP & CPAP machine to help me breathe. I ended up on oxygen for a year afterward. It literally was a miracle I survived! Statistics say there is only about a 10% survival rate from A.R.D.S. I count myself so lucky I was one of the 10%.

I will never forget that experience, but it made me appreciate life more; mine and my daughters. I am thankful I was given a second chance at life, and my daughter was unaffected physically. She is healthy, and happy!

I thank all who prayed for me and were there for me and my daughter during that time, who helped take care of my Maddie when I couldn't. They know who they are.

purpose driven/ free to be unapologetically me

14

Narrative for 2015
(Hope/Letting Go/Loneliness Returns)

The following poem is about being lonely after having my daughter and almost losing my life- the challenges I was facing raising my daughter as a single mom during this time, and still recovering from A.R.D.S.

How I longed for friends and support, and since I left the father of my daughter, I was back to square one, looking for love. Even still I was so thankful for the birth of my daughter, which is the most precious of any love.

I had always wanted the full package- a husband and child. It was a good start to my future family, though I realized and knew in my heart there was still love out there for me, just on the horizon…

purpose driven/ free to be unapologetically me

2015/Hope, Letting Go, Loneliness Returns

The Unseen
I fear for the days that have passed me by
No one around
To see me laugh or see me cry
Memories of my life have passed me by
Times in my youth
Where I had wings to fly
I wake up each day for hope anew
But I go to bed, just singing the blues
I put on my best, hoping to be seen
But I look around and realize it was only
A dream
I don't even recognize this world we live in
What happened to stopping by to see a friend?
Sometimes I'm afraid the light within me
Is getting dim
I dream of throwing a party for everyone to see
Hey, it's ok to be next to me
I'm the same girl you knew with a bright smile
And big dreams, a heart for good, and talents unseen
If you ever get a glimpse of this girl you once knew
She's the same today as she was back then
Just anxiously waiting to see what lies ahead
There's no more time to keep
Looking back at what I have lacked
Moving onto the straight and narrow path
What's gone is gone, time swept it away
But with the light of each new day, I will continue
To pray and believe
For the bright and blessed miracles coming my way

15

Narrative for 2016
(Victor)

I met Victor when I was 19 and heavy into the rave scene. This was when I was experimenting with ecstasy and Ketamine the most. We even lived together in a party house at one point. He was someone I cared for very much and I always had a crush. He and I always had a love for one another and became friends with benefits throughout the years, both dating other people in between of our love flings.

He and I lost touch for about 10 years throughout my recovery from drug addiction and mental illness, my struggle with obesity, and my fight to regain my identity. Victor and I reconnected through social media around 2012. He lived two hours from me, however, so we still didn't get to see much of each other. But when we did, we always had a good time and shared our love for one another. He was my best friend, and I was happy to be receiving desperately-needed love and affection!

Victor and I did have our struggles, though, and he was never actually single, even though he and I were going through a fling. I was in love and he was unavailable to me. This hurt me deeply. There was much time in between when we didn't get to see one another, and my heart would ache. We always kept in touch through text, and when he could, he would take a trip to come see me or I would go see him. He was my best friend and someone I could confide in and who took away the loneliness.

I will never forget the day in November 2016. As explained Victor wasn't always available to me so I found other routes of comfort through online dating, even though I still was looking for love and never really found the right one.

Free to be unapologetically me

During this time I had been talking with someone online who lived out of state. He ended up ghosting me, and I was very hurt because he and I were really starting to get to know each other.

I remember one night in particular Victor and I were talking through text. I had been drinking and feeling lonely and wanted to relapse. Victor too struggled with heroin addiction.

He told me he was holding and to come pick him up. I remember being about ready to head out the door when something told me not to go. He had text me prior to tell me he was stranded at a 7/11. And when Victor needed my help, I was always there for him because we had a long history and I loved him. So right before I was about to leave, he texted me a second time and told me he was going to be in a room at a motel. He told me the whereabouts of this motel, and that I was to pick him up there.

Immediately, I was scared! My heart was pounding and my stomach dropped. I looked up at a picture of my daughter, who was staying with her grandma that night, and I had a revelation at that very moment! Something inside me warned me not to go! That if I left that night I'd never see my daughter again! It was the Holy Spirit talking to me! So I listened and climbed back into bed.

This was to be the last time I ever heard from Victor. A couple months later, I learned of his passing. To this day, I still don't know how he passed as he and I were not friends on social media during that time. I just happened to go to his page one night and saw it said "Remembering Victor." I fell to my knees in disbelief! I was horrified, and to this day, I wonder if it was that same night that he died and why I had the feeling not to go get him!

I also struggle with guilt that maybe I could have saved him, but deep inside I truly believe I would have also died had I went. I miss him every day and the next poem is about him...

Bernadette Padgett
2016/Victor

Too Young to Die

Nostalgia that drives me insane
Wanting to re-capture the good old days
Oh' how times have changed
Memories like mini snap shots in my mind
People come and go
Time after time
It's those that become a part of my soul
I will remember for a lifetime
While I wander this world alone
Never really knowing which way to go
I remember your smiling face and the times we shared
It warms my heart to know you're still there
I catch myself looking
Down at my phone wanting to send a quick hello
It's heart breaking that you're not here
But I see you in my dreams
And your spirit will always live on inside of me
Because you are a part of me
I miss you so much; this world is so corrupt
I imagine the end of my days, even
Though it would be hard to say goodbye
It's sometimes where I want to be
Because then I'd get to be with you for eternity
But it's just not my time
So I keep trudging through this life
Hoping one day it will all make sense
Because that is when in my heart I can rest. I love you so much
and now you know because
In Heaven you can't deny what's in your soul

purpose driven/ free to be unapologetically me   2016/Victor

I see you flying free in perfect peace
And I'm so thankful to have a loving angel
Watching over me!

R.I.P. Victor/I love you B.F.F.

16

Narrative for 2017-2019
(Toby)

Toby and I met in January of 2017. It had only been a few months after Victor's passing. I was so heartbroken and consumed by sadness. I'll never forget shouting at God in my kitchen, asking why he had to take my best friend! I missed Victor terribly, and once again, felt all alone.

With tears streaming down my face, I started to pray, asking and pleading with God to bring me a new best friend. My heart ached and I needed comfort. I said something along the lines of "Lord, I am at the end of my rope. Please bring me someone new who will love me, be there for me, be my new male best friend, and possibly become my husband." "And if not, then please just take me!" "I don't want to be here anymore without the love of a best friend, and eventually, my husband."

A few days later I tried a new dating site and this is when I met Toby. I'll never forget what stood out to me on his page; he too loved star gazing and was looking for true love! This matched my heart and we began to talk. Come to find out, Toby and I had much in common. We built a strong bond and related with one another on so many levels! I truly felt like he was my soulmate!

We dated for about a year, and then we finally became an official couple. We had many ups and downs as we both struggled through financial and family difficulties. He also was a recovering heroin addict and suffered from brain damage after a severe car accident a few years before. He was pronounced dead on arrival, ended up in a coma, which caused brain damage. You'd never be able to guess from talking to him face to face, as he functioned normally.

purpose driven/ free to be unapologetically me

As the relationship went on, Toby was using and kept it hidden from me for some time even though I had my suspicions. He finally told me. He had lost his job and his home and I decided to let him move in with me. Now knowing he was using my drug of choice, even though he made promises to me to get clean, I too started once again in my addiction. We experienced some of the most beautiful, tender love I could ever hope for, but it wasn't all rainbows and butterflies.

He continued to stay on dating sites while we were together, which hurt me tremendously. We both wanted to get clean but we struggled through the detox and being sick and needing to get well to function and work so we wouldn't lose my apartment.

Eventually we both ended up on methadone. We couldn't afford our habit, and we needed to be well to go to work. It worked for a short time, but he and I were not doing well on the methadone. I ended up having a bipolar episode and I noticed changes with him too. He was becoming very angry and aggressive with me. He became violent, often punching holes in walls, damaging my property, and he ended up hitting me a few times. At this point, I knew I was in trouble and was having thoughts of leaving him.

By 2018, we were seeking relationship counseling through the methadone clinic. After the first appointment, it was raining on our way home, and Toby was driving. He lost control of the vehicle on the freeway and we hit the wall! I was severely injured! My ankle was shattered and my ribs were broken. I was in the worst pain of my life! Thankfully, Toby was ok.

I had a long journey ahead for my recovery. I ended up having to endure two surgeries, and learn how to walk again! I was in and out of hospitals and rehabilitation centers for my ankle.

Bernadette Padgett

I eventually went home to Toby for a while and he took care of me, but he was still using and showing signs of rage, verbally and emotionally abusing me. There was a particular incident he threatened to kill me with a knife in his hand. I feared for my life and left him. I ended up in a group home and Toby moved out.

I wanted to work things out with Toby, but at the same time I was afraid of his rage episodes and the domestic violence situation I had become a victim of. I never thought in a million years that this would happen to me with everything I saw happen to my mom growing up!

Toby and I remained in contact by phone, and he eventually returned home to live with his parents up north. My doctor said it would take two years for a full recovery from my ankle injury, and I was wheelchair bound for over a year. I went through intensive physical therapy and it was a very painful journey.

I eventually got my life back, and got a new car, and new place. I tried my hardest to stay away from Toby, but I still loved him even with everything we had gone through. We reconnected later once I was in my new place. Again, he needed my help and a place to stay. He wanted to get out of where he was staying, which was basically on the streets since his parents kicked him out for using.

I let him stay for only a couple months when, once again, his abusive behaviors started and so did the using. I had told myself I had been through too much to go down this path again and I wanted no part of the drugs or the abuse, so I ended up having him arrested and removed from my apartment for criminal damage.

I went several months with no contact with him. We did get back in touch later, but several other instances took place. Eventually he made it into a sober living, and is doing much better. I am very proud of him!

Toby and I had a complicated love story we were both hurting and struggling with our own demons and mental illness. All in all, he is still my best friend and I will always love him. He has a special place in my heart, and even though we don't see each other anymore, I wish him the very best! And who knows what life will bring. Maybe we will reconnect and be able to have a healthy friendship with healthy boundaries. Maybe not, only God knows. Most importantly, I want him to take care of himself, and love himself, and stay clean, just as I need to do the same!

Two broken people who struggle to love themselves and end up in a relationship are usually bound to fail (Sad to say). We both realized we have to work on ourselves before we can have anything else including a relationship. And that's exactly what we're doing.

The following poems reflect the love we shared and my feelings for him…

Bernadette Padgett
2017-2019/Toby
(A Complicated Love Story)

Mirror to My Soul
Searching, yearning on this journey
Through life.
When you've seen it all, but in your soul
You know there's more to explore.
When you've walked alone
Year after year
Shedding millions of tears
But no matter how dark life's been
In your deepest, secret, heart-of-hearts
You always knew there was a true friend.
Someone out there who understood without explanation
And with no reservations
Someone that in their loving presence spoke
The same language.
A happy-go-lucky friend who taught me
How to smile again
He who took me by the hand and gazed into my eyes
With a look so hard to describe
A look that said it all, no words necessary
Because it was a new way of connecting
When I shared a part of me
Your gaze captivated me
A lost and lonely girl who only knew deep sorrow
Who wanted to give up,
But still kept showing up
Because she believed in her dreams she was
Being shaped into God's
Masterpiece.
It's the magic and song in her heart

purpose driven/ free to be unapologetically me

2017-2019/Toby
(A Complicated Love Story)

"Mirror to My Soul, Cont'd"

That kept her going through this life.
She pictured you
In her mind time after time
And she knew you in her soul way before
It was time to meet
She always knew there was someone out there
To sweep her off her feet
Which she could see with you staring back at me
I'll never forget the day
You took my breath away
Valentine's Day to be exact. I shared my tears,
My hopes and fears
You took to me because you paid such close attention.
Sharing my deepest pain with you by my side
And the look of love deep within
Your eyes
Made it all bearable like a flash back through time
You walked next to me like an angel
Illuminating the darkness of night
I see your purity within
And with just one glance you lit up my life
Which helped to close that dreary chapter which your
Spirit made alright
No more pain, suffering, or mistreatment
You deserve to endure true beauty
Which the heavens poured out from your eyes
Enormous amounts of hope

Bernadette Padgett
2017-2019/Toby
(A Complicated Love Story)

"Mirror to My Soul, Cont'd"

And sunshine
So beautiful I was swept away
You came into my life and took the pain away
My spirit was asleep and with every ounce of love, gentle kiss,
and your presence, it woke me from a living dead
I don't know where this life will end
But I do know where the journey began
Hope anew I am alive again!
Because of you!
You swept the pain away and told me I'm ok
I cherish you dear friend
My angel in disguise, lighting up my life
I love you because you brought my dream to life
My best friend till the end
Thank you honey for saving me from the darkness
My knight in shining armor, Prince Charming
Your strength and love taught me to rise above
And allow myself to live again
A love deep within you will always be
A part of me
Our spirits shine bright, I know there's
More to come because a love like this can't be undone
A miracle you are; the one I'd been waiting for
Always and forever, an angel
Sent to me from above
I've never known this kind of love
Eternally grateful, because God sent me my earth angel
I love your smile and your tender touch

purpose driven/ free to be unapologetically me

2017-2019/Toby
(A Complicated Love Story)

"Mirror to my Soul, Cont'd"

And all that you stand for
You were the angel at my door
Society can be so mea
Please don't be afraid to walk next to me
This is more than
Just a dream.
The perfect outer package I may not be
But a love so genuine
This is the real me.
You must look deep
Within to realize the meaning
Of a true best friend
I love you till the end!

Eternally Yours,

Bernadette

Bernadette Padgett
2017-2019/Toby
(A Complicated Love Story)

A Love like Yours

Live it, Love it, See it, Dream it, Believe it!
Life is a dance
I dream of romance. My soul
Cries out, just give me one more chance!
Stay strong, stay beautiful
The words of an angel
Feeling the emptiness while praying for a miracle
Thy lyrics in my mind
My heart goes blind. I see you in my heart
And I wish we didn't have
To part
A piece of my soul I leave with you
I didn't want to leave you
Memories flutter
In this life we all suffer
I'll dream of you always, my best friend
My desired husband
One last look, before I close this book
A memory in my heart implanted in my thoughts
Foot prints on my soul
But I had to let you go.
As we dance in the rain, please God heal my pain
I'll forever see you; The Beauty of God's grace
In the sunlight seeping through the clouds

purpose driven/ free to be unapologetically me

2017-2019/Toby
(A Complicated Love Story)

"A Love Like Yours, Cont'd"

In the moonlight shining down, I will always remember you
And be proud I got a chance to experience you
Love like an angel
An answered prayer
Thank you for loving this broken girl
A love so soft and gentle
I prayed for you even before I met you
May God forever bless you
Bright as the stars above
A young love
Peace be with you always, you were my one and only
Love and dance like
No one's watching.
Live it, Love it, See it, Dream it, Believe it!
I set you free
Thank you for loving me
When I couldn't see clearly
In my heart you will always be with me

Forever Yours,

Bernadette

Bernadette Padgett
2018-2019/Toby
(A complicated Love Story)

 Lost Love I Set You Free

This heart- break's brought me to my knees
Pain I never knew; a heart that bleeds
I don't think I can endure
When I want to see the sunlight, but all I can do
Is cry
Painful memories keeping me up at night
You were my one and only
A mirrored image to my soul
Thought you'd never hurt me, thought
You'd never let me go
Believed our love was real; I hurt so much
Beyond what I can feel
Joy is a dream just out of my reach
Just not quite enough needing
You to love me
Do you still think of me like I do you?
Catching glances in our dreams
Souls united, do you
Still feel me?
I never wanted to let you go; now I sit alone
Lost and lonely longing
To be held
Afraid to die alone in this living hell
What happened when I fell?
Did you pick me up?

purpose driven/ free to be unapologetically me

2018-2019/Toby
(A Complicated Love Story)

 "Lost Love I Set You Free, Cont'd"

No, you knocked me down
Shattered glass of painful memories
This love brought me
To my knees
With nothing left but a hole in my heart
I'm haunted by images
Of you in my mind
I tried to save you so many times!
But we just didn't have the strength to put up the fight!
I hope one day I see you
Living a happy life
I understand more than you know
And a place in my heart you will forever be
Especially when I kneel down to talk to God
And hit my knees
I hope to see your smiling face
When the memories were sweet
Those are the times I cherish most
Between you and me.
In my heart the memories will always be
Times when we rode the waves
Of insanity
Combined with moments of Heaven which
Impacted my life
Often times I dreamed of becoming you wife
But I guess that's a long lost dream

Bernadette Padgett
2018-2019/Toby
(A Complicated Love Story)

 **"Lost Love I Set You Free, Cont'd"**

No matter what in spirit, may your
Soul rest with me
I loved you like no other
And often times had to be a mother
Keep your child-like
Dreams, and know how much you
Mean to me!
I wish you comfort in your trials
And pain
May you overcome your fears and be free
I hope you'll be happy
And thank you for teaching me
About heavenly love
Even though the road was often tough
I'll see you in my dreams
Where I can rest in your embrace
Where the pain is no more; and our souls can endure
In my heart forevermore
A lost love, but a lesson it taught
I wish you well Toby Bear

Bernadette xoxo

purpose driven/ free to be unapologetically me

17

Narrative for 2019
(What Matters Most)

This section of my book is all about what it is titled, "What Matters Most."

I've had to learn the hard way in this regard. What I realize with everything I've been through is that; it's not about my size, what I look like, who accepts me, or what society thinks of me. It's all about learning to love and accept myself, and not need others approval. To walk with my held high and be proud of whom I am!

I have learned a lot through my trials and mistakes, including things I've been through that were not my fault, but a victim of circumstance. Although I do take full responsibility for the poor choices I've made in the process and the consequences I've had to face.

Life is not easy, but I can say I am a better person for having lived through so many tragedies! It was pointed out to me just recently by a good friend, the story in the Bible about Israel and their people God promised to take to the promised land, and originally God had intended for it to only take days, but it took them forty years later to make it with almost the entire generation of men who had died.

I take notice to this story in the Bible because I will be 40 years old this July and only now have I lived up to my dreams of writing my book! I know everything happens for a reason and in the right season, so with that being said I'm thankful I have received God's promise to me to fulfill my destiny.

Forty years it took, but I had to survive all the tragedy to be able to share it with the rest of the world! I am thankful God is in control, because he is the reason for my life and all glory goes to him! The following poems reflect my take on life and what's most important to me…

purpose driven/ free to be unapologetically me

2019/What Matters Most

Looks Can be Deceiving, Striving for Believing

I see the way this world looks at me
With its ugly eyes
Always telling lies, judging me by my size
With their evil laughs
And devilish glares
There's nothing to compare
A beautiful soul living free
It doesn't matter what they say about me
Because my body image
Is my testimony
It's ok to have scars and some
Extra love hugging those curves.
Without them I might merely be as worldly and shallow
As everyone else tends to be
Living out a fake fantasy
So what if I hobble when I walk
I'm thankful these legs can still
Hold me up
Cripple? Maybe a little…
But I'd take that any day than being spiritually
Crippled and a slave to worldly ways
I've been to battle many times
But it doesn't mean I will give up this fight
Fall I may, but being a true warrior for my Lord and Savior
Nothing will ever keep me down!
I am a princess crowned and heaven bound
So laugh if you will with those ugly glares
There's nothing to compare

Bernadette Padgett
2019/What Matters Most

"Looks can be Deceiving, Cont'd"

I know I'm not perfect, but going to let my
Light within keep shining
Always keeping in mind God's timing
The first will be last, and the last shall be first
Given this life I strive to
Do what's right
My creator in Heaven has got my back
Therefore there is
Nothing I lack
Given a second chance there is no
Looking back
I know I'm on the right track
Heavens light is shining down
Holding up my crown
No evil laugh or ugly glare is ever gonna get me down!
I'm proud of who I am
Living for my Savior, walking hand in hand
With my creator
Beauty is within so forget what this world says…
I'm happy to be living this life
Holding on tight, praying, believing, and
Doing what's right day and night

purpose driven/ free to be unapologetically me

2019/What Matters Most

Spending Time With Jesus

Goodness I seek so I no longer have to weep
Oh' what divine mercies
He has bestowed upon me
The other night I laid down to cry myself to sleep
And as I did this, I heard the Lord speak to me
He said with stretched out hands
Here, take my hand and come follow me
I saw a tree with a stump so thick
As if God were showing me his strength within
Jesus and I decided to take some time
So we walked along the oceanside
Our bare feet in the sand while he lovingly held my hand
And at one point when the pain was so deep he picked me
Up when I could no longer walk
Just like a father would do for his child he loves
He set me on a rock so I knew it was he
Who keeps me strong all my days long
While I experienced day after day
Of heartache and pain; loneliness and sadness
Waiting for my companion
For he knows the desires he put in me
He told me to weep no more
To surrender to him because he's already got him picked
As Jesus and I continued walking side by side
I asked the Lord when?
He smiled and said in his perfect divine timing
I felt his presence strong and felt delightful
Indeed picturing myself as a giddy child
Jesus went on explaining this to me

Bernadette Padgett
2019/What Matters Most

"Spending Time With Jesus, Cont'd"

He said you must keep going
You must endure all things; you never have to walk alone
Again in darkness or uncertainty
For I am the truth and the light
And I will bring you comfort at night
So dry your eyes and be glad; I've got you in
The palm of my hand
Come and see, he said to me
As we walked through the open door
And he poured out his blessings upon me
I asked Jesus, can you show me the way?
To rid me of my pain and afflictions that get in my way?
He said, dear child, I've already prepared the way
Never look back just take my hand
I will comfort you; you may rest your head on
My shoulder; my love for you endures forever!
Jesus spoke and it gave me hope
I asked Jesus to give me a new perspective and
Understanding that he would reveal himself to me
And oh what a blessing I received!
Because in all my pain and wallowing
Jesus spent time with me
Revealing his love for me; I even got to picture him
On a mountain top
And there I was with his other disciples
Learning of his abiding love
So I asked myself....***What matters most?***

purpose driven/ free to be unapologetically me

2019/What Matters Most

"Spending Time with Jesus, Cont'd"

Temporary pleasures through worldly temptations
And the flesh?
Which only leads to darkness and dismay
Or crying out to Jesus in my
Loneliest of night
And getting to experience a new understanding
Of his mercy and light?
In all my being I pray to be more like him
My desires can no longer
Be of this world, instead I gaze
Upon the sunset at the seashore
With Jesus showing me a better way to be
Happy, whole, and hopeful
And to continue to hang onto the light
Of the dawning of a new day
When the sun rises and smiles upon your face
I will be thanking sweet Jesus
For the time he spent with me
Jesus loves and endures all things, Lord
Knows he's put up with a lot from me
Jesus wipe my slate clean
That I may have a new hope
And a new
Understanding

 *In Jesus Name,*
Amen

Bernadette Padgett
2019/What Matters Most

The Best of Me

Dodging evil glances and ugly stares
I may shed tears
But you can't get the best of these years
Once upon a time
Those glares destroyed me
Now I use them to fuel me to be a better me
And to never lower myself to such
Mediocrity
I learned a long time ago we can't change the world
Around us; but we don't have
To let it define us
People are people and they will hate
But don't you dare think you know me
When you haven't even spent a moment with me
Alone I may be and the pain inside
Is deep; but maybe there's
A purpose I'm still here standing on these two feet
It's easy to feel lost
In a world you know you don't belong
Bitter hearts everywhere you turn
But looking up, I know God's doing
So much more and giving me purpose
Which is what defines my worthiness
This world thinks they
Know me; sizing me up and down
With their glares; but who cares; if they truly
Knew me they'd embrace me
Because inside we all look the same
And that's when we start to care

Pain is pain and doesn't have a face

purpose driven/ free to be unapologetically me 2019/What Matters Most

"The Best of Me, cont'd"

It's the wounds we carry stamped
With heartache on our souls
While someone like me
Carries the cross all alone
I don't understand; I don't know why trials
I face over and over
Will there be a time the load gets lighter?
Where instead of sorrow
A miracle takes over?
Seems like I'm holding out forever
Being buried alive by these trials of life
Is there an end where I can look in the eyes
Of someone who understands
Who bears the same cross and knowingly
Is able to lift me up?
I long for a soul to unite
Who won't take advantage and hurt me
Time after time; night after night
Someone who doesn't want to take
Just wants to pour out their heart
And embrace the
Broken-hearted, the lost and forgotten
I long for my partner in life that will make
My burdens light
Who helps me smile again and have a
Reason to hope, lost I've been for years and years
Suffering in great sorrow; nursing these tears
Trying so hard to believe God hasn't forgotten me

Bernadette Padgett
2019/What Matters Most

"The Best of Me, cont'd"

To walk the ups and downs and know
They'd never leave my side
Someone who doesn't care if I'm the perfect size
That I don't need to fit the perfect mold
Because they fell in love
With my soul
Maybe there's still a chance
This can't be all in vain … holding on day after day
For someone to walk in the rain
Stare at the stars above
And know without a doubt this is true love
Maybe someday, someway
I will meet my earth angel to dance in the rain
It's been over 20 years
I've endured this pain of the waiting game
God I'm growing old and weak
Please hurry and bring me the man to
Sweep me off my feet
Who will get down on one knee and ask me to marry thee
Oh' what I wouldn't give to meet my one and only
And discover a new purpose- filled life!
It's life or death; I've been put through so many tests
I've endured so much pain and lack
Please give me a chance to get my life
Back on track holding on by threads
As I anxiously await the day I meet my
Soulmate, to love and share and complete this life
And overcome these trials in life!

"The Best of Me, cont'd"

And no longer care
About the ugly stares
One day before long it will be over and done
Hope it's soon as God
Puts me back on my feet
And introduces me to the
Companion he has for me and
A father for my Maddie
I will give it one more day
As I continue to wait
And ask the Lord to take my pain away
Heaven knows
I've given it the best years of my life
He is the only one who knows just how
Hard I have tried

Bernadette Padgett
2019/What Matters Most

Mini Snap Shots

I sing till there's no lyrics left to sing
I cry till the streams are bone- dry
I hurt like no other
But I also laugh, and love like the inventor
Of it all
What's done is done; I feel as though
I've lived through it all
Been there, done that at only 39 years old
In the same breath; on the contrary
I also feel like an infant
Seeing the world for the first time
Youthful excitement for all things new
Hoping, searching, and believing
The world is good and then reality
Says silly child that's only a dream
And closes that door
Nothing left to explore; nothing left to do
One minute you're tying your shoes
Next minute you're dying
No need for shoes
This isn't my first rodeo; and I'm sure
It's not my last
Funny how time repeats itself;
In an instant flash! Here today, gone tomorrow
I guess what's important is the in-between
Hold onto those special moments
And the rest let float away in the stream
The stream of life; that's what this is

purpose driven/ free to be unapologetically me

2019/What Matters Most

"Mini Snap- Shots, cont'd"

Rifts and ripples are inevitable
But it is ever-flowing; and that's what's incredible
Here today, gone tomorrow
Borrowed time
With mini snap- shots in my mind
To freeze those special moments, we only
Wish could last a lifetime
Those moments are what's closest to my heart
If I could push repeat I would, just to feel
It all over again
Those timeless moments bring tears to my eyes
The passion, love, and happiness
That truly is the prize of
Life!

Bernadette Padgett
2019/What Matters Most

Glass Shadows

Can a shadow be breakable?
Seemingly, no
But what if those shadows resemble the pain in your soul?
It follows you around day after day
A contrasted image from the sunlight's rays
Can a shadow feel?
It depends on its stance
Can it show power? Pain?
Just from taking one glance?
What's the significance of a shadow after all?
Some are big, some are small
But one thing holds true…
It belongs to only you
You can't judge a shadow just by looking at the ground
What it feels, what its worth
But I can tell you this…your shadow has significance
Watch as children play,
Happily chasing their shadows day after day
Believing they can catch it, or making their shadow puppets
Joyously enjoying the images on the wall
If children can enjoy this sort of thing so much,
There must be significance after all
Many often wander through life and forget to embrace
Something so small
But children have a way of enjoying even the smallest of
Things, like their shadows on the wall
Something as adults we often forget to take a chance and
A glance to look and see

"Glass Shadows, cont'd"

So the question still remains…
Is a shadow breakable?
To me it is; metaphorically so
If you allow life to get the better of you it will show
All around even amidst your shadows on the ground.
You'll also forget the joys of your youth
Like your shadow puppets, and what it's worth to you
And that's when your shadow becomes
Breakable like glass
Because you've forgotten your power stance!
To stand tall and upright,
And even splash in the puddles through
The journeys of life
Your shadow is unique, embrace it, and remember
It's just below your feet
Does your shadow show happiness
And that you are free?
Or does it show sadness and great defeat?
Your shadow is your friend, embrace it,
And make it dance again!
Go out in the daylight and try it, and you're
Sure to smile again!
Don't ever let it be breakable or shattered like glass!
Remember your true self, and let
Your shadow resemble that!
That's truly the image I seek to last and last
And why my shadow has significance
An image I wish to keep close to me
Which is the real me
And will always be what matters most to me

18

Narrative for 2020
(Purpose Driven)

The final chapter of my book is where I touch on my God- given life purpose! So much I've learned and realized through this life. God planted a desire in my heart to share my story, and while I put it on a shelf for many years, I am so thankful I decided to go for it!

Throughout my walk with God, one thing I always remember reading in scriptures is that God will take our worst tragedies in life and use it for the good of others. This is how I found my purpose in life! I have hands- on experience through multiple challenges, and I have the knowledge through those experiences to help uplift others.

The most effective teachers are the ones who have the experience and lived through it to share with the rest of the world! I am forever thankful for that!

The following poems reflect my determination to strive to achieve greatness in this life, to overcome, and leave my legacy to the ones I love, especially my daughter!...

purpose driven/ free to be unapologetically me

2020/Purpose Driven

Carpe' Diem

Do it! Do it now!
Life is filled with ups and downs
No time to wait; it's not worth the escape
Pain comes with growth
So never give up hope!
Get up and be proud; it's up to you
Or this world will surely bring you down
Simplify those thoughts in mind
And surpass the mountains
You aspire to climb
Reach out and live
We all have something to give
Peace be with you
Love it, live it, and
Be who you are
Run that race and chase those dreams
It's time to overcome those obstacles
Of uncertainty
Life is filled with lessons learned
Be brave, be bold
And your triumph will be told
This legacy is yours
Embrace it and courage will lead you
To new and open doors
So always remember to seize what is yours!

Bernadette Padgett
2020/Purpose Driven

Straightening My Crown

I never felt like I mattered
Like I ever fit in
Hard to live in my own skin
Mortified by the glances around me
Is what I'm seeing real?
Is this how life's supposed to feel?
Is it how I see the world? Or how the world sees me?
Does it really matter when
At night I kneel by my bedside to hit my knees?
God is the only one that truly knows,
Loves, and accepts me
Life is like a dance; taking it step by step
One minute in perfect rhythm and harmony
The next, a lost footing
Which makes way for tragedy
What does it all really mean?
Breathless, lifeless, a burden so deep
Waiting for someone to
Sweep me off my feet
A moment of sweet ecstasy
Followed by years of self-afflicted misery
Like a record on repeat
I'm a woman of purpose; driven by my dreams and
Lessons learned through great defeats
I really don't know what it all means but hoping someway,
somehow my life will turn upside down for the better
Long-awaited dream coming to pass

*Straightening My Crown, cont'd"

This is my last chance!
I'm ready, willing, and free
This is my time to live fully!
Nothing stopping me!
A poetic soul; stepping into the unknown
What better
Time than now
To rise up; and straighten out my crown
So thankful for the journey
I am on now!

Bernadette Padgett
2020/Purpose Driven

Living Out Loud

Water flowing gently through the stream
Life is precious
For every human being
I skip to the sound of my own heart beat
Laughing at everything I see
Will I go up? Or will I go down?
Every day's a challenge; just take the time to look around
Be careful with each step;
For you might only have one last breath
Laugh when you can
And cry when it hurts
And live each day like
It's your last on Earth
The day is awesome and I am too
Because every day is something new
Bitter sweetness is what I mean
Because I'm finally living my life-long dream
Shout it now! Shout it from the rooftops
Live out loud, an unapologetic self!
The time is now!
Get up, get out!
Get your life on track
It starts with that single step
Embrace who you are
And put down that crutch
Life is what you make it; there's no more giving up!

purpose driven/ free to be unapologetically me

Victory

The first will be last; and the last will be first
It does not matter
If I'm favored on Earth
My story lies within my scars;
And now that I'm living for the Lord
Heaven is not too far
Many will seek the wickedness
Of their own ways
In all actuality; they have made themselves slaves
Slaves to unhappiness and defeat
I pray for them to humble themselves
And get on their knees and seek
Seek the goodness and mercy of the Lord
For the world will swallow
You up; if you forget to look up, which is better?
To be a master of your own selfishness?
Or become a servant of God's
Everlasting love and holiness?
Everyone has the right to choose
But if you choose your own will, you will surely lose
I encourage all to be brave in these last days
We are at the final countdown
Where God and the devil settle the score
Choose love, choose life;
Because there will be a time when you no longer
Get to decide
Do what's right because your decision

Bernadette Padgett
2020/Purpose Driven

Victory, cont'd

Will affect your everlasting life
Or are you choosing strife?
Let it be known who so ever surrenders his will
Will be the ones to overcome
And victory will be for all to see
Because in that he will be free
And will have defeated the enemy!

Choose Life

  Happiness is not a final destination. It is amidst the daily struggles, in finding hope and perseverance. In your daily decision, strive harder than the day before in each moment, and in faith. Doing that is when we see God's miracles through our trials.

  It's in the not giving up and choosing to smile through the storms. Knowing whole heartedly that the sun will shine again, giving us hope, strength, and clarity to continue to rise each and every day.

  In this process of life we experience the joys, sometimes so suddenly, and out of the blue, we can only recognize it's in God's doing in which he made our hearts anew. We, through all our efforts and hard work and believing, become gifted with moments of God's heavenly blessings touching our lives and souls. A glimmer of hope to the pained and afflicted.

  Hold tight to those God- gifted graces. He has a timing for everything, and he will make your burdens light. Happiness is sure to find you in the inner workings of your precious journey to Heaven's beaming light of an everlasting life!

Bernadette Padgett
2020/Purpose Driven
Insight

My God-Given Purpose

I've got stars in my eyes
What a sweet surprise; living a Christ-centered life
There's no stopping me now
Heavens angels cheering me on!
Been picked up from the ashes
Reborn to a life of ever-lasting happiness!
Curtains up, my time to shine
Thankful for this life of mine
Truly a dream- come- true!
I am over-joyed with seeing what God can do!
When I simply let go, and trust
And choose to live my best life now
This is what's real; and I've waited a lifetime
To feel
This triumph and victory over me
Makes me unstoppable
I surely am a walking miracle!
God never let me go
And sharing with the world
Helped me overcome what was truly
Meant for tragedy
Is now my greatest victory!

purpose driven/ free to be unapologetically me

Bernadette Padgett

2020/Purpose Driven
In Closing

    Thank you for letting me share my story- what was, what happened, and what could have been. How I overcame to live my best life now! This is not the end, because my story is continuous...living it a day at a time, a remarkable journey full of love, hope, happiness, and praising God for His glory over my life!

    I would not have survived without him, and as I continue to shine, there will still be days I stumble. But I am so thankful none the less, because I choose to live my life humble.

    Embracing life for all it's worth, I am blessed beyond measure and I cherish each and every day because all we really have is the moment. Make it memorable and always believe in your dreams! And when in doubt, hit your knees!

    Don't have a faith-failure! Walk in your divine destiny! Don't let your conscious be de-sensitized by sin! Keep that conscious within! Let it continue to shout! It's there to protect. Never let sin win! We are all meant to overcome!

2020/Purpose Driven
In Closing

I hope this book has brought some insight through the sharing of my life's struggles, expressed in a creative-form, through my poetry. If you are a non-believer, I encourage you to ask God to make himself known to you and pray.

He is always there and truly cares! It's never too late to seek forgiveness and repent and ask Jesus to be the Lord of your life and your personal savior. It will be the best and most important decision you will ever make, and through that, you will experience amazing things! I'm living proof!

God Bless You All!

Love, Bernadette M. Padgett
X.O.X.O.

"True beauty in a woman is reflected in her soul"

-Audrey Hepburn

"Nothing is *impossible*,"
The word itself says
"I'm Possible!"

-Audrey Hepburn

www.ingramcontent.com/pod-product-compliance
Lightning Source LLC
Chambersburg PA
CBHW062022290426
44108CB00024B/2741